eman

imity

a state of psychological stability and composure which is undisturbed by experience of or exposure to emotions, pain or other phenomena that may cause others to lose the balance of their mind.

THE
CO-CREATIVE AGE
THE NEXT EVOLUTIONARY PHASE IN LEADERSHIP

Sally Anderson

RHG | MEDIA PRODUCTIONS™

RHG Media Productions
25495 Southwick Drive #103
Hayward, CA 94544.

Visit us on line at www.YourPurposeDrivenPractice.com
Printed in the United States of America.

National Library of New Zealand Cataloguing-in-Publication Data

Anderson, Sally, 1965-

The co-creative age : the next evolutionary phase in leadership / Sally Anderson.

ISBN 978-0-473-69411-1

1. Leadership. II. Title.

658.4092—dc 2 23.

For my sister Kirstie Anderson,
who passed in February 2014.
I so miss you – thanks for being my biggest
cheerleader, sis!

OF THE KORU

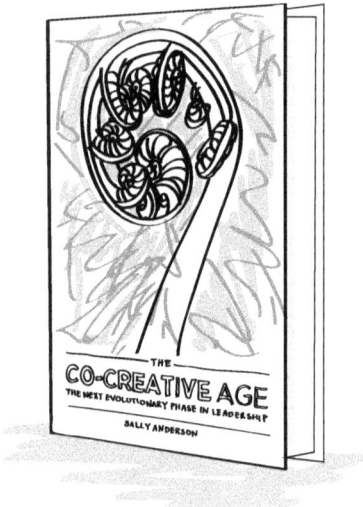

In Māori design, the koru has a dual meaning. It is commonly used in Māori art as a symbol of creation because of its fluid circular shape. Based on the unfurling fern frond of the native New Zealand silver fern, the circular shape of the koru conveys the idea of perpetual movement, while its inner coil, the corm with rolled up inner leaflets, suggests a return to the point of origin. In the larger scheme, this is a metaphor for the way in which life both changes and stays the same.

HARMONY

Some have determined that the koru meaning is one of harmony. Between the chaos of change and calm of the everyday, there is a point of equilibrium, a state of harmony in life. In its balanced shape the koru represents this.

NEW BEGINNINGS

The koru is also said to represent new life. Literally speaking, the baby fern frond slowly unwinds over its adolescent lifetime as it grows into a mature frond. It then opens into a brand new leaf on the silver fern plant where it ages and then dies. This is the fern frond's life cycle. When the silver fern leaf is a frond in its life cycle, it's a baby; therefore people associate the koru design with new life.

What People Say

Sally Anderson is one of the most effective transformational coaches on the planet. In my opinion, she's as good, if not better, than Anthony Robbins. If you want permanent, life-altering results, and have tried everything else, call her!

Paris Cutler, Blue Ocean Strategist, Sydney, Australia

"Leadership is such a loose word in the 21st century. We all know we need a new model. We all know the current fear-based, command-and-control model operating since the Industrial Revolution does not create an inspired, co-creative network of people within our cultures.

Sally Anderson has a unique and powerful way of reshaping the core (the leadership) of an organization, and then expanding that core to such a degree that the cultural DNA is changed forever. Her understanding of the human psyche, and her ability to use this insight to reconfigure the way in which leaders lead, place her as one of the greatest leadership influencers of our time.

Sally Anderson is bold, she is courageous, and she is a futurist. Her work is a game changer for those who seek to propel their companies and teams to new heights.

To lead, one must understand and have been the follower; to heal, one must have experienced and embraced pain; and to transform, one must be willing to shed the very skin that has constricted them for so long.... this is Sally Anderson! Her incredible depth of intellect, her ability to connect intuitively both environmentally and internally, and her unbridled drive to help transform the leadership of this planet, are awe-inspiring.

The Co-Creative Age is a must read for every leader who intuitively knows that the time has come … a new era of leadership has begun."

Terry Hawkins (CSP), Founder, IGNITE Humans

"Sally Anderson is, without a doubt, one of the most influential thought leaders in the personal transformation space of our generation. Her talents and techniques change lives around the world."

Steve Lowell, past president of Global Speakers Association

"There are many voices in the world of leadership. So many that one could describe it as a cacophony of noise. Every now and then a fresh sound emerges from that mosh-pit of sound and distinguishes itself through authenticity and truth, often brutal, but yet still very essential.

Sally Anderson is a fresh, vital voice in the world of leadership. She is not everyone's cup of tea because most people will not be able to stand the exposing heat of transparency, vulnerability and exposure that Sally brings with her. I've known, worked with and been coached by Sally. I know what I'm talking about. Sally Anderson is the real deal!

I've been in the audience when Sally has 'live coached' a room full of experienced business leaders and saw transformation in its purest form – emotional rebirth – take place. I've seen both men and women lose the facade of pretense and literally shine with the peace that comes with being real... being true... being who they were designed to be... authentic leaders with a mission worth pursuing.

Those principles that I've seen demonstrated and proven in the cauldron of this kind of reality are what you will experience in this latest, essential work from Sally Anderson, *The Co-Creative Age : The Next Evolutionary Phase In Leadership*.

If you are a leader of people, the highest and most prestigious of Callings of all Callings, please do your people and yourself a favor. Read this book! If you know someone who leads people, then I encourage you to help them become better ... more effective ... more vital as a leader! Give them *The Co-Creative Age : The Next Evolutionary Phase In Leadership* by Sally Anderson and see them change themselves and their world."

  Eugene Moreau, Founder, Eugene Moreau Consultancy

"Future leadership does not resemble past leadership. What's more, no-one can help you evolve, to make the difference you were supposed to make on this planet, better than someone who has spent a lifetime helping people prove to themselves just how much impact they can make.

In a world crying out for great change, Sally Anderson delivers equal measures of evolution and revolution in this pivotal inflexion point in leadership education.

If you feel like you are destined for more, for a bigger game, to fulfil a calling, Sally Anderson is *the* one to get you there. Read this and read it again and again.

Leadership is no longer something you do alone. Our world has evolved, and so too can leadership on this planet. The queen of sustainable transformation has spoken and we would do well to listen very carefully."

  Paul Broadfoot, Founder of Paul Broadfoot Consultancy

"Rare is the leader who can surrender to those they are leading …
Sally Anderson's voice and rare insight are ushering us gracefully into
the next level of self-awareness, and conscious global stewardship."

Danielle Lin, C.N. renowned lecturer and health educator, creator
and host of the US nationally syndicated talk radio program,
"Danielle Lin … The Art of Living and Science of Life"

Futurist Sally Anderson is a quintessential equanimous leader who
is an expert in decomposing complicated personal transformational
challenges and organisational leadership complexities to simplicity. I
have hundreds of great leaders and coaches in my circle, but a few
things differentiate Sally from the others–her authenticity, tenacity,
originality, passion, and results. As an advocate of co-creative
innovation, I have never seen anybody so versed in co-creative
leadership and the transformational journey of self-mastery like her.
The first time I listened to Sally's coaching, my jaws literally dropped
to the floor–I was mesmerised!

Benjamin C Anyacho, MBA/PMP LION Founder, Austin, Texas

"One of the great privileges of life is the wonderful people we
encounter along the way – I have met many such and one of my
absolute favorites is Sally Anderson. I went to her training to learn
and came away as a friend. Her gut-wrenching personal journey belies
the delightful person she is; she will challenge you and love you all in
the one breath, and she always inspires me to be the best version
of myself.

Late last year I hosted Sally to do some training with my company and
just yesterday I was quizzing one of our guys about his operations
when he explained to me, 'Oh, when we have to make a decision, big
or small, we always Sally Anderson it.'

There are lots of people out there with a powerful message, but Sally does one thing better than all the rest – Sally Anderson walks the talk and that is truly inspiring."

Alan Cooney, General Manager, Topx Australia

Table of Contents

Acknowledgments

Finding the time to write a book takes something as a leader when championing a global vision. So the first acknowledgment goes to Gihan Perera (at GihanPerera.com) for his wizardry in providing a seamless book-writing process that is nothing short of masterful.

To my husband Roger Eugene Te Tai who passed August 2021, thank you for enabling me to experience a love most people only dream of. Although you may not be here in physical form, you are with me every day in spirit and I know your presence fuels my entire being—I miss you beyond words!

To my cousin Vicki Walker, for your wonderful creative genius and illustration work for this book.

To my clients and those that have experienced the Co-creative Leadership education in its various forms, thank you for trusting your intuition and honoring your legacies which make such a profound difference on the planet.

To Andrew Mackay, one of the most loyal friends, stalwart supporters, advocates, cheerleaders one could ask for. Thank you for your unwavering belief and support.

To Paris Cutler, thank you for being part of my journey, for your mentorship, friendship, direction, guidance, selfless contribution to my calling.

To Kathryn Porritt, thank you for being the extraordinary human that you are and for the legacy leadership you administer to many every day. You are an earth angel.

To Michelle Mortlock, thank you for your financial mentorship, guidance, support, and priceless friendship; you were heaven sent.

To my faith, for the life apprenticeship you provided to enable me to teach and pay forward the lessons learned.

Foreword

When Sally asked me to write this foreword I was both challenged and excited. I am excited because in my opinion Sally is one of those extraordinary people you only get to meet a few times in your life. That's saying something: my business Thought Leaders means I get to spend an inordinate amount of time around people that are truly inspiring and making a difference. No doubt Sally's backstory is point of difference enough – anyone who has been thrown the life lessons and dramatic experiences she has would be someone worth listening to – and yet that's not her greatest asset. Sally has taken a life's worth of experience and added a life's worth of learning and teaching the idea of rigorous self-responsibility.

Sally is a powerful creator and as such the perfect person to write a book about the co-creative age. This book should read like a codebook for hacking the future. It's rich and it's layered. The equanimous leader concept alone is an idea that should cause deep meditation and reflection in any leader who is exposed to it.

In Mahayana Buddhism, *bodhisattva* is the Sanskrit term for anyone who, motivated by great compassion, has generated *bodhicitta*, which is a spontaneous wish to attain buddhahood for the benefit of all sentient beings. Reading this book I feel like that Sally is a modern-day bodhisattva, a rare soul who pauses on her journey to enlightenment to ferry others across the river of consciousness.

The Co-Creative Age unpacks a theologically agnostic view for creating companies and cultures we would all be happy living and working in. The ideas within this book are accessible to the agnostic, atheist and extremist. I was a fan of Sally's first book *Freefall – Living Life Beyond The Edge*, and am happy to say even more so one of this book. It just might be Sally's life opus. That said, I have learnt that – WOW – is never a full stop with Sally. So don't read this book – absorb it. To elevate consciousness on the planet is the greatest and most worthy job any teacher can undertake.

Matt Church
Author of *Amplifiers: The Power of Motivational Leadership to Inspire and Influence*

ignite

AWAKEN A SENSE OF URGENCY, AROUSE INTRIGUE, FUEL PASSION FOR WANTING TO EXPLORE THE UNKNOWN REALM

"We need enlightenment, not just individually but collectively, to save the planet. We need to awaken ourselves. We need to practice mindfulness if we want to have a future, if we want to save ourselves and the planet."

Thich Nhat Hanh

1

THE CRAZY
ONES

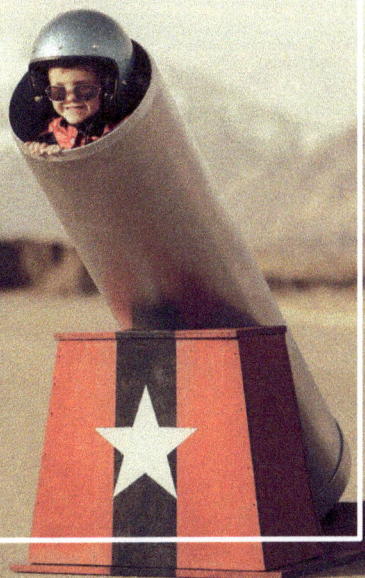

"History shows us that the people who end up changing the world – the great political, social, scientific, technological, artistic, even sports revolutionaries – are always nuts, until they are right, and then they are geniuses."

John Eliot

I am here to reaffirm you are not crazy or nuts. You are just called to follow your bliss, as Joseph Campbell says in *The Hero's Journey*. When championing a vision, there are many trials and tribulations you have to overcome along the way, including the naysayers, the judgers, the assessors, and others who criticize what you are doing.

For many years, I could not understand why things were not working. Why wasn't traction seamless? Why did other people's journeys always seem far easier than mine? I didn't realize at the time that, as a visionary, what you view as *not* working is actually part of the apprenticeship in preparing you for what you are here to do on planet Earth.

When you are at the leading edge of thought and pioneering something new, personal sacrifice is part and parcel of your apprenticeship. Hindsight is a wonderful thing. I now realize it could not have happened any earlier – because I was being prepared. The journey of learning to turn your belief into a knowing takes perseverance, stamina, and conviction beyond your human form. The zillion No's were fuel for the fire for that one Yes that made it all worthwhile.

When you are still looking for evidence, you question your belief. When you realize your calling has its own time dimension, you come to know it cannot but be accomplished when you learn the art of true surrender to what you are being called to do.

We all have a responsibility to evolve to our highest potential in our human existence. Whether you fulfill on this in this lifetime is up to you.

When Joseph Campbell wrote *The Hero's Journey,* he researched every aspect of mythology, every philosopher, and every thought leader in psychology. He distilled this into the Hero's Journey: a twelve-step journey to transformation – which I'll describe later.

Every leader, every entrepreneur, and every seeker cannot but follow these steps.

It is undeniable that everyone has a calling. We all hear the call – but whether we listen to it or not is debatable.

In my opinion, there are three groups who hear the call.

1. You Hear The Call But Deny It

The first group hear the call, but deny it. They think it's weird or stupid, or are swayed by the naysayers and critics. They doubt themselves and ignore their calling.

When they get that intuitive tap on the shoulder, they ignore it. When they get hit by that 4-by-2 at the back of the head, they still ignore it. Then the Mack truck experience arrives!

That wake-up call might come in the form of redundancy, bankruptcy, a child dying, cancer scare, or even acts of God.

When you're stripped of everything, or left completely out of control, you certainly get to know who you are in the world.

2. You Hear The Call And Act On It

The second group hears the call and decides to act on it. They embark on the journey, leaving behind what they know, and start the transition into the unknown. As *The Hero's Journey* describes, they go through trials and tribulations, face many tests, and find helpers and guides along the way.

Many of them stumble because they still have evidence-based thinking. Evidence-based people are waiting for evidence to show up before they trust – they are "I'll believe it when I see it" people. But when you move into the unknown, you operate from trust, not evidence. Trust-based people know evidence is the reward for trusting implicitly.

There's a period of time when you are challenged, questioned, and asked to ignore the evidence (or lack of it) and act on trust and belief. This is just part of the journey.

In his book *The Tipping Point*, Malcolm Gladwell researched and documented the "tipping point," when something – a person, an idea, or a product – seems to transform magically. He discovered there is no magic formula for reaching a tipping point; it just happens when the right things combine in the right way at the right time.

This happens on the Hero's Journey as well. Some people won't reach the tipping point, and will give up and go back into the known realm. They find the Hero's Journey too challenging, so they choose to abandon it.

3. You Hear The Call And Accomplish Your Bliss

Those who persist on the journey will eventually "tip." They have a spiritual awakening and a transcendence in their understanding of their calling. They look back on their trials, tests, and tribulations, and realize they are just part and parcel of the process.

Part of the journey is realizing you're being prepared, and that every "No" and adversity along the way are wake-up calls for you to transcend your limited thinking into unlimited thinking.

Along the journey, it's easy to make judgements about what's working (and what's not) from the limited realm of the known. But to make the transition, you need to let go and trust, and then you can look back from the unknown realm.

I've worked with hundreds of leaders over the years, and I know the tipping point is always there for those who persist. At some point, you can't *not* tip!

After that, belief and trust become knowing. When that happens, you own your presence and step out of the trenches to do what you're here to do – and play the game at the level you're being called to play.

This is the transition from the known realm – with all its limits – to the unknown realm – which is limitless.

When you get a taste of living in the unknown realm, trusting your intuition, you know the mission is bigger than you are.

If you're called nuts or weird or crazy, take it as a compliment. Those who judge you have no concept of the unknown dimensions, and they will never achieve the heights of what is possible in their human existence.

Never Give Up!

A high percentage of leaders I know have never heard of the Hero's Journey, but they recognize it when I describe it.

If you're reading this now and know you're being called to something bigger, decide what path you will take.

You can deny the calling and stay in the system, because the system feels safe and comfortable, while embarking on the journey is risky and uncomfortable. But don't wait for that Mack truck to hit you!

Or you might be actively in progress with your calling, but keep coming up against challenges, tests, and trials. It's tempting to judge them from your human perspective, and see them as too hard. But never, never, never give up, regardless of what's thrown at you.

There are 8.1 billion people on the planet, and most of them won't go on the journey of self-discovery. So they live in the known realm, relying on evidence, and disassociated from the limitless possibilities of the unknown realm.

I ask you the question today: What do you think *we* could do to have more awareness around evolving in our human existence in this lifetime? It doesn't have to be a scary experience. Instead, it can be one of the most exhilarating journeys you will ever experience!

It's Time!

When you were a child, you trusted implicitly, and you had unlimited possibility. Then you became conditioned, and your world became smaller, with evidence-based thinking and fewer possibilities.

Now it's time to explore the unknown again.

Even if you're doubting, resistant, and yet to be convinced, you can just take a look.

Look at the world and you can see a quickening going on – in business, in politics, in social interactions, and in ourselves. We need a new kind of leadership, based on co-creative values and new levels of consciousness. We have a responsibility to have a sense of urgency, to follow the call.

Here's To The Crazy Ones

You might remember Apple's famous 1997 advertising campaign, which included these words from Rob Siltanen, the head of their advertising agency:

"Here's to the crazy ones. The misfits. The rebels. The troublemakers. The round pegs in the square holes. The ones who see things differently. They're not fond of rules. And they have no respect for the status quo. You can quote them, disagree with them, glorify or vilify them. About the only thing you can't do is ignore them. Because they change things. They push the human race forward. And while some may see them as the crazy ones, we see genius. Because the people who are crazy enough to think they can change the world, are the ones who do."

These words were the foundation of one of Apple's most successful marketing campaigns. They are also the call to those who choose the Hero's Journey.

It's Tried And Proven

◣

Here is the Hero's Journey, as outlined by Joseph Campbell, an American scholar who analyzed narratives in storytelling, myth, drama, and religion. He discovered they all follow the same pattern, which he distilled into twelve stages.

The story describes the adventure of The Hero, who embarks on a journey to achieve great deeds on behalf of a group, tribe, or community:

1. **The Ordinary World:** The Hero is living an ordinary life, unaware of what lies ahead.

2. **The Call to Adventure:** Something disrupts the comfort of The Hero's World. The Hero is called to action.

3. **Refusal of The Call:** The Hero feels the fear of the unknown and refuses the call, preferring to rely on the safety and comfort of the known world.

4. **Meeting with The Mentor:** The Hero meets a mentor who provides guidance to dispel the doubts and convince The Hero to take the journey.

5. **Crossing The Threshold:** The Hero leaves the safety of the ordinary world and starts the journey into the unknown.

6. **Tests, Allies, and Enemies:** The Hero is tested and meets both allies and enemies along the journey. Each helps The Hero prepare for greater obstacles yet to come.

7. **Approach:** The Hero and newfound allies prepare for the major challenge in the unknown world.

8. **The Ordeal:** The Hero faces a major ordeal or severe crisis, and must use all their skills, knowledge, and resources to face this challenge – and conquer it.

9. **The Reward:** After conquering the challenge, The Hero seizes the reward and heads home.

10. **The Road Back:** The Hero faces one last challenge on the way home, and must overcome it in order to ensure the reward or treasure can be returned safely home.

11. **The Resurrection:** The Hero is severely tested again, and this final battle often requires a last sacrifice. Ultimately, The Hero succeeds, emerging cleansed and reborn.

12. **Return with The Elixir:** The Hero returns home bearing the reward that has the power to transform the world.

It is with utmost admiration that I dedicate this chapter to those yet to follow their bliss, those currently championing their bliss, and those who have accomplished their bliss. I salute you all.

Rest in the *knowing* that you are the geniuses, you are the ones who will change the world!

"We must be willing to let go of the life we've planned so as to have the life that is waiting for us."

Joseph Campbell

This is not just a leadership book. It's an iconic book dedicated to the evolution of the human race as we know it. My entire purpose for being is to lead and evolve in the Co-Creative Age. If some people view me as one of the crazy ones – a nutter – I embrace this fully as part of my path to being viewed as a genius in my field.

Recommendation

It is undeniable that as a human being, you will be called. We were all born with free will, so it is your *choice* whether you follow the call!

I *highly* suggest you watch the excellent movie *Finding Joe*, which you can find at FindingJoeTheMovie.com.

It's an inspirational movie on what it means to "follow your bliss."

2

THOSE WHO HAVE
GONE BEFORE

There have been many visionaries and pioneers over the centuries who have had to transcend in order to follow their calling and achieve what they came here to do. If they had not stayed the distance, we would never have evolved to where we are today.

These are people from all walks of life: scientists, artists, entertainment personalities, authors, political leaders, and business leaders. It's not their chosen career that they have in common; it's the fact they choose to follow their calling.

Here are a few examples of these pioneers and visionaries.

Thomas Edison

Edison was the most prolific inventor in American history, with over a thousand patents in a wide range of fields, including telecommunication, electric power, sound recording, motion pictures, primary and storage batteries, mining and cement technology.

Edison is famous not only for what he achieved, but also for his hard work and persistence. He famously said,

"Genius is one percent inspiration and ninety-nine percent perspiration."

His determination and persistence in the face of trials and tests is even more evident in another famous quotation:

> "I have not failed 10,000 times. I have not failed once.
> I have succeeded in proving that those 10,000 ways will not work. When I have eliminated the ways that will not work, I will find the way that will."

Oprah Winfrey

Oprah Winfrey was born in the backwoods of Mississippi to a single teenage mother. She had a difficult childhood herself, being raped at age nine, and giving birth at age fourteen to a son who died shortly afterwards.

From these challenging beginnings, she rose to fame in the entertainment industry, from radio presenter in high school to her own daytime television talk show – the highest-rated TV show in American history. She is worth over $1 billion, and her philanthropic work helps women and children worldwide.

Bill Gates

The former technology entrepreneur, currently the richest man in the world and a philanthropist investor, dropped out of Harvard University because he "couldn't bring himself to go to class."

He founded Microsoft with John Allen in 1975, and took on technology giants like IBM to bring computers – which until then were only large, expensive business machines – into ordinary households.

Gates retired from Microsoft in 2008, and now works tirelessly with the Bill and Melinda Gates Foundation to seek solutions to the world's biggest problems.

Steve Jobs

Like Bill Gates, Steve Jobs left college when he felt he was not going to find his true calling there, with "a hope that it will work out well."

He teamed up with engineering wizard Steve Wozniak to create the first Apple computer, which also accelerated the growth of the personal computer industry. Despite his success, he was kicked out of his own company in 1985, but returned 12 years later to save the company from ruin. In his second stint at Apple, he spearheaded a renaissance led by the creation of the iPod, iPhone and new generations of Mac computers.

Walt Disney

Walt Disney is a cultural icon throughout the world, who changed the American animation industry and spawned a multi-billion-dollar empire that all started with an animated mouse.

He had a number of false starts to his career, including having to shut down his first animation company, losing the rights to his first animated character (Oswald the Rabbit), and being rejected by MGM when he wanted to promote Mickey Mouse (because MGM executives thought a giant mouse on screen would terrify women).

J.K. Rowling

Although Joanne Rowling graduated from Exeter University, she struggled early in her career. After her divorce, she had custody of a daughter, and struggled on welfare to raise her small family. She was diagnosed with clinical depression and contemplated suicide.

Her first book, 'Harry Potter and the Philosopher's Stone', faced rejections from twelve publishers before finally being accepted. It was an instant success, and led to the sequels that were even more successful. Currently, she is one of the richest women in Britain, and a philanthropist.

Lee Iacocca

Born to Italian immigrant parents in 1924 in Pennsylvania, Iacocca grew up learning about business from his father, who was a cobbler, restaurant owner, and theater owner. His engineering degree secured him a job with the Ford Motor Company, and he became vice-president in 1946.

Despite many marketing successes at Ford, he was dismissed in 1978, and moved to Chrysler. During his time there, he transformed Chrysler from a sluggish giant to a nimble, highly profitable business.

Richard Branson

Branson, best known as the founder of Virgin Group, which comprises more than 400 companies, was another success who struggled with formal education (partly because of dyslexia), and dropped out of school at 16.

He launched a youth culture magazine, and in 1970, he set up a mail-order record business. In 1972, he opened a chain of record stores, Virgin Records, later known as Virgin Megastores. Branson's Virgin brand grew rapidly during the 1980s, as he set up Virgin Atlantic and expanded the Virgin Records music label.

In March 2000, Branson was knighted at Buckingham Palace for "services to entrepreneurship." In July 2015, *Forbes* listed Branson's estimated net worth at US$5.2 billion.

Michael Jordan

Jordan is widely considered to be the greatest basketball player of all time. He led the Chicago Bulls to six NBA titles, and was declared MVP (Most Valuable Player) five times. On the world stage, he helped the USA win gold in both the 1984 and 1992 Olympic Games.

"Some people want it to happen, some wish it would happen, others make it happen."

Michael Jordan

Although he had many successes, his journey also had some serious trials. After his father was murdered in 1993, Jordan retired from the game. He returned to sport via baseball, and then switched back to basketball the following year. He retired again – and made yet another comeback – before finally retiring in 2003. Since then, he has been involved in many charitable organizations, leveraging his name and fame to support disadvantaged youth.

"I've missed more than 9000 shots in my career. I've lost almost 300 games. 26 times, I've been trusted to take the game-winning shot and missed. I've failed over and over and over again in my life. And that is why I succeed."

Michael Jordan

Mark Zuckerberg

Mark Zuckerberg was famous for founding Facebook while at Harvard University, but his initial foray into it was less successful. His first social media site, Facemash, was shut down because its popularity overwhelmed the Harvard computer system. Frustrated by this obstacle but pleased by its success, Zuckerberg dropped out of Harvard and, together with some friends, moved to Palo Alto to continue building Facebook.

His original plan was to expand it to other universities and then to high schools, but he struck gold when Facebook opened itself up to everybody. Today it has over 1.5 billion users – larger than any country in the world, and with no sign of stopping any time soon.

The List Goes On

So what's my point? We can learn a lot from those who have gone before. So why the resistance to follow that which you are called to do in this lifetime? Is this not enough evidence that those who persevere win?

Evolution only occurs if we learn to *trust the unknown realm* from which we were born. This subject doesn't appear in standard traditional leadership teachings, nor is it a prerequisite in our education system. It should be!

Key Learning

As humans we are wired to wait for evidence to show up before we trust. Yet, as I have mentioned, those who trust the unknown know the reward is evidence.

Where in your life are you waiting for evidence to show up before you take action?

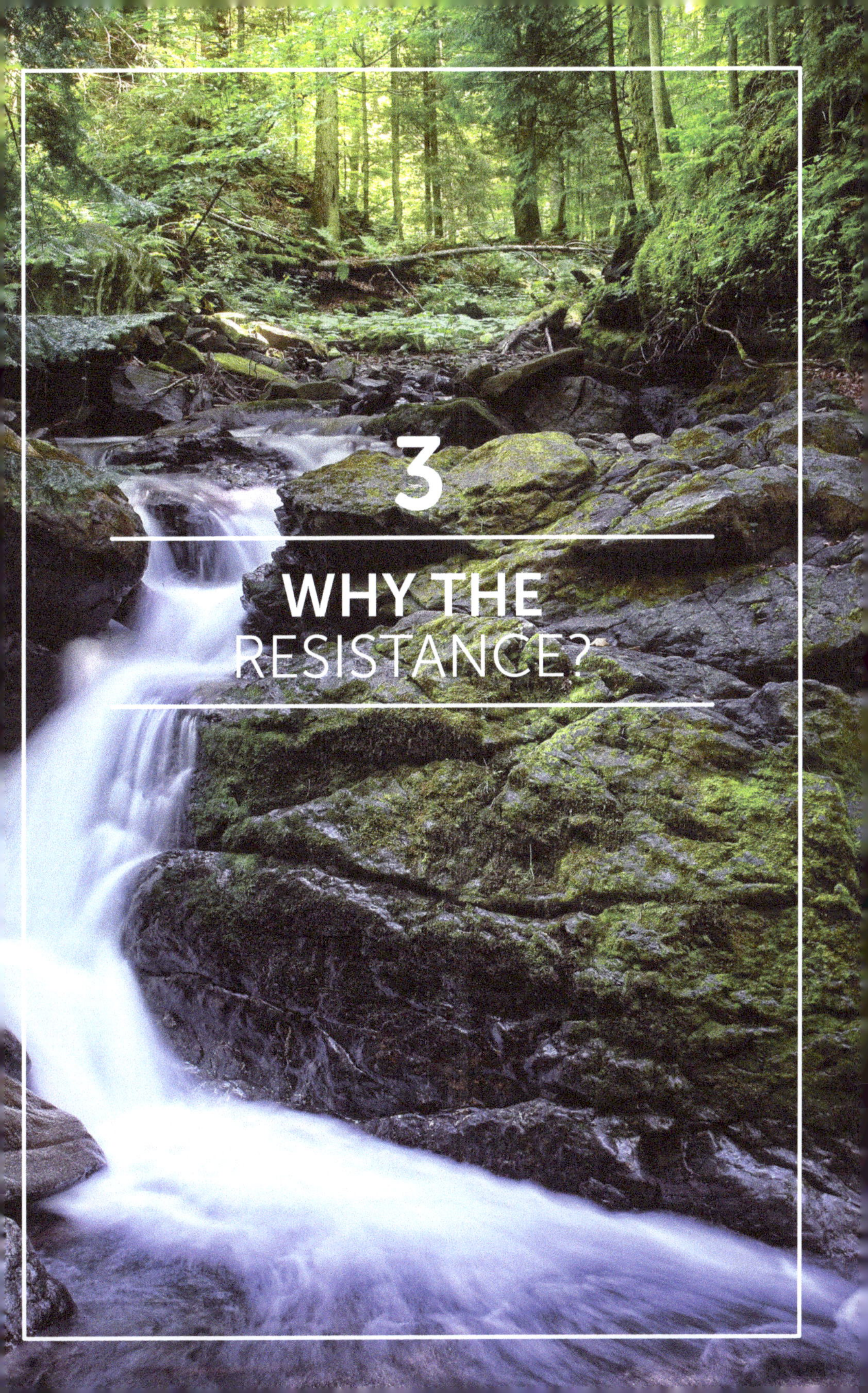

3

WHY THE RESISTANCE?

Why is there resistance – even *vehement resistance* – in the business world when we use the terms faith and spirituality?

These words are usually collapsed into a religious context. Don't get me wrong; I have nothing against religious faith, and I'm not denigrating it in any way. I've had the privilege of coaching people from all sectors of faith, religions, and spiritual doctrines, and even atheists. From my perspective, I totally honor whatever the individual believes. However, with respect, I think most people are completely and utterly inauthentic and hypocritical to their faith, because they don't walk it.

I'm a spiritual teacher, teaching people to walk in a way that they never have before, and to transcend their identity as they know it.

When I use the terms spirituality and faith in this book, I'm talking about trusting the unknown realm as much as the known realm.

That's it!

In the corporate context, I intentionally avoid putting a name to it. Whether you call it a higher power, universal force, collective consciousness, or God, I just say, "Trusting the unknown implicitly."

You might wonder what "trusting the unknown realm" really means. Human beings have an instinctive need for safety. We learn from an early age not to trust ourselves, others, and the world at large. Every human being is born trusting implicitly, and then learns not to trust. To re-access this realm – this experience – we need to learn to trust again.

To automatically discount the power of trusting the unknown is completely and utterly negatively impacting our ability to evolve as a human race.

Think about that for a moment.

You Are A Product Of Childhood Beliefs and Values

CEOs often ask me, "Sally, when I come to see you about my business, why are you talking to me about my childhood?"

It's a fair question with a simple answer. Beliefs and values are adopted in childhood, and we learned these beliefs and values from teachers, parents, siblings, and the environment. Some empower us and some don't.

Our beliefs and values drive certain behaviors, which in turn drive the structure of our actions, then the structures drive the culture, and the culture drives the results.

As adults, people try to incorporate change from the outer layers: culture and results. They say, "I want to lose weight" to fit into the cultural norms, or, "I want to change our organizational culture." They expect to get results (especially lasting results), but rarely do.

If there is to be any level of sustainable change, you need to go back to the original wiring of where the beliefs and values originated.

If I don't facilitate a conversation with a leader about the source of their original programming – which they're not even consciously aware of – then that will play out unconsciously within their lives (at a huge cost).

The impact on one individual who is unconscious is big, but it's massive when you consider it collectively within an organization, which is made up of many human beings.

I am not interested in dragging up a leader's past, but I am committed to them understanding themselves wholly and completely, so they can achieve the magnitude of what they are here to accomplish. When you unearth disempowered beliefs and values that affect your behaviors, structures, culture and results, you can create sustainable, lasting change individually and collectively.

You Have A Disempowered Default Identity

Everybody has what I term a "default identity," which is an identity that defaults to disempowered thoughts and experiences.

Moment by moment, human beings operate from one of two states: the empowered state or the disempowered state. Our conditioning means we have a tendency to default back to being disempowered.

The ability to transcend this default identity is a function of two things: understanding it and then getting clear about what it's costing you. This gives you the motivation to create a new identity, which is the empowered identity. When you reach that level, you no longer need to oscillate between empowered and disempowered states.

Now look at how this plays out in organizations …

If we believe that in every organization there are human beings (hardly a novel concept), and every human being has a default identity, then that creates a series of (disempowered) default–default relationships, which in turn create a collective (disempowered) default culture.

In the business and corporate world, most people operate from the known realm, because they don't trust the unknown realm. There is an urgent need to educate those who lead to trust the unknown realm implicitly.

Why Is Faith Often Collapsed Into Religion?

The default identity likes to play it safe. When faced with a challenge, it will automatically go to an extreme and discount the possibility. It never accepts new evidence (unless it confirms an existing belief), so "same old, same old" plays out.

When it comes to "faith," it's easy to collapse this into something you already know: religion. You can then dismiss it, either as something you already know or as something you don't respect or understand.

I don't mean in any way to diminish the value of religion. If you are religious, then faith already has a strong meaning in your life, and I totally respect any leader who walks that faith. However, many others use "religion" as a convenient excuse for dismissing anything to do with faith. This is your default's reaction.

It's only when you consciously bypass the default identity – and the decades of conditioning that created it – that you can open your mind to faith being trusting the unknown realm.

Leaders are unconsciously competent when it comes to traditional leadership philosophy: the hard skills and left-brain concepts. But when it comes to soft skills and right-brain concepts in the arena of belief and behavior change, they are usually sadly in deficit. Most leaders are highly trained, yet most don't experience the level of transformation they want, nor know how to sustain it. That's because they don't know they have a default identity that holds them back.

Dismissing faith as "just religion" is purely a function of your default behavior. The word "faith" is misconstrued and mistrusted, and few in the business world see it as integral to their evolution, individually or organizationally.

The Cost Of Being So Afraid

Most human beings are so afraid of the unknown. And yet it's the key missing ingredient in our leadership training, education system, communities, societies, and governments.

There are 8.1 billion people on the planet, and most are disconnected from the present. They are either living out in future-based projections – creating worlds that aren't even here yet – or dragging in something from the past (past-based projections). They're hardly ever present. To live a connected existence, learn to live in the present moment. That is all we have, yet we are rarely here!

A Model For Faith

When I ask, "Is this *it* for you?", most people respond, "Oh, no! Not yet, anyway. When I get the house, the boat, the man, the woman, the car, the promotion, the salary target, etc., then it will be *it*."

The opposite of having faith is the requirement for evidence before you trust.

On page 31, you'll see a model for faith.

In brief, this shows the default (disempowered) identity on the left and the power (empowered) identity on the right.

You're either in your power (right-hand side) or you're in your default (left-hand side).

At any time, you're the balance of the two sides – living at a high or low level of consciousness, heart-based or head-based, connected or disconnected, acting without evidence or forever waiting for evidence.

Faith-based people implicitly trust, knowing that evidence is the reward. Evidence-based people, on the other hand, are waiting for the evidence to show up before they trust (Don't hold your breath)!

You have access 24/7 to a limitless power, but – because of your disbelief – you're not accessing it. It's like having Lotto available 24/7, but some people just aren't collecting the winnings.

If you're operating from your default – the disempowered state – you're living at a lower level of consciousness. Your thinking goes like this:

- **Confusion or Resistance:** You stay in total confusion because you don't know what to do (stuck in the "how") or you do not believe at all.

- **Distrust:** You distrust due to parental conditioning and other past-based events.

- **Confusion:** The evidence doesn't arrive (How could it, when you didn't take any action to find it?), so you're still confused or disbelieving.

- **Frustration:** As a result, you tell yourself "I told you so!" and get frustrated at the lack of change, or it becomes a self-fulfilling prophecy because you did not believe.

When you operate from your power – the empowered state – it's a higher level of consciousness. In this state, your thinking goes like this:

- **Action:** You follow your intuitive voice and take action, even without the evidence (yet) to support it. You may not understand it, but you are open to exploring.

- **Belief:** You start believing it's possible, regardless of internal resistance or external skepticism.

- **Trust:** Your belief builds trust, which in turn leads to …

- **Evidence:** The evidence that spurs you to take more action, which in turn validates your belief.

If we believe we were born intuitive, connected and fearless, it makes sense that we need to return to this state in order to access limitless possibilities.

How Convenient You Are So Confused!

Confusion is a function of the default. How convenient that you're confused! It means you don't need to take responsibility. You don't have to look!

People operating from their default say, "I don't believe in something that has no evidence." They don't trust the unknown, so they bring up evidence from their past – their upbringing or whatever other excuses as to why they don't trust – all stemming back to childhood. Usually, most use a past-based experience where they trusted and it didn't work, so they default back into confusion and distrust.

Ontology (the study of "being" human) has shown that separation generally started between the ages of three and five. After that time, it's easy to find evidence why you shouldn't trust. But if you don't trust, you can't access the limitless possibility of the unknown realm.

POWER

- Higher Lever Of Consciousness
- Heart Based (Emotion)
- Evidence
- Limitless Potential
- Attracted to the Unknown Realm
- CONNECTED

Possibility/faith based people implicitly trust knowing the reward is evidence

Lotto

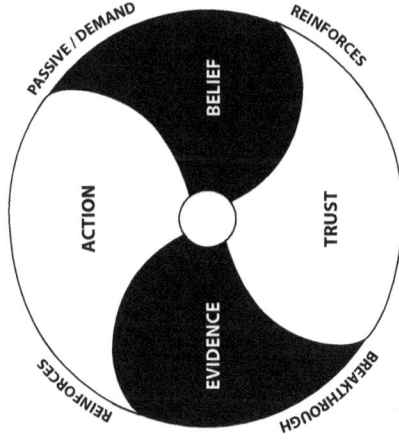

PASSIVE / DEMAND — REINFORCES — BELIEF — TRUST — BREAKTHROUGH — EVIDENCE — REINFORCES — ACTION

CHOICE

DEFAULT

- Lower Level Of Consciousness
- Head Based (Thoughts)
- No Evidence
- Limited Potential
- "Attached" to the Known Realm
- DISCONNECTED

Evidence based people are waiting for evidence to show up before they trust

Not Collecting The Winnings

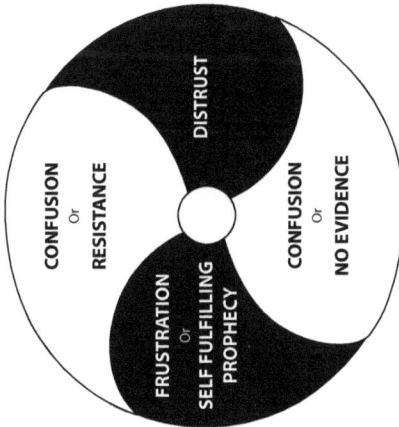

CONFUSION Or RESISTANCE — DISTRUST — CONFUSION Or NO EVIDENCE — FRUSTRATION Or SELF FULFILLING PROPHECY

FAITH MODEL

If there's distrust, you will stay in confusion, and then there will be no evidence. That then leads into either frustration or a cycle of self-fulfilling prophecies.

Action Leads To The Evidence

Obviously you won't find any evidence if you're hanging out in confusion, and obviously you won't find evidence if you have limiting beliefs. If you believe you can, you can; and if you believe you can't, you can't!

Of course, most people find it difficult to transcend their default identity. So do you want some evidence? Just a tiny bit of evidence that there might be some legitimacy to what I'm saying?

Here it is in one word: *Action*.

Only action will give you the evidence.

This works even if you're cynical. It works – even in the face of your cynicism or skepticism – because taking action will give you some evidence contrary to what you thought.

Cracking The Code

I have cracked the code on how to have people find the evidence they need to feel safe enough to trust again. It is my life mission to impart what I have learned.

All I ask is that you do not automatically write off a possibility before you try it. If you start with the intent of wanting to find fault and disprove it, that's the evidence you will find. But if you put your disbelief aside for a moment and *act as if it will work*, it will work!

If you don't take action, you'll never find the evidence. When you do take action, it's the first access point to the possibility of evidence showing up.

As the model on page 31 shows, action leads to belief. When your belief starts to shift, energetically other things shift as well – particularly what you attract and what you see. This then builds trust, and then the evidence appears.

Little Boys And Little Girls Running The Show

Have you ever noticed we have a lot of little boys and little girls running businesses, economies, and countries for they have NOT done the 'deep soul work' on themselves.

You might not like words like "healing" and "faith," but the fact is most leaders don't have enough awareness of these concepts. If you are human, you are not devoid of the need to reintegrate back into being whole and complete – regardless of how good your childhood was.

We separated at a young age and it takes something to return home.

By "separated", I mean we learned not to trust! We were born intuitive, fearless and connected, but as we take on beliefs, values, and behaviors from our parents, teachers, siblings, and the environment, we separate from our unique essence.

Leaders have a responsibility leading human beings. Being unaware of these concepts affects each person – the leaders themselves and those they lead. This in turn affects our economy, our society, and the world as we know it.

Without a doubt, awareness-based training needs to be an integral part of evolving leadership capability.

Bring On The Skeptics!

Over the past two decades, I have specialized in working with leaders, and I have witnessed extraordinary transformation from those in leadership positions who have accepted healing as an integral part of their leadership responsibility. The most skeptical, shut-down, non-believing CEOs have taken my advice. The result: evidence!

It's OK to be cynical or skeptical. Embrace that, because it only demonstrates how disconnected you are from yourself and from that which created you.

Which Stage Are You At?

There are three distinct stages of awareness evident in our society today:

- **Stage 1:** Do not believe – and committed to finding evidence to validate this belief

- **Stage 2:** Believe, and do their version of walking their faith, whatever that is for them – but still fearful

- **Stage 3:** Believe, walk their faith, and benefit from leveraging their co-creative ability

There's nothing wrong with any of these stages, but my concern is their impact on evolving consciousness as we know it. Instead of resistance to exploration, I would love to see rigorous debate and an openness to entertain a new possibility. The challenge is that the default identity denies any other possibility because it is deemed to be unsafe.

Leaders are human, and most humans don't trust. If traditional leadership remains focused on the known realm alone, we are not leveraging what is possible in the unknown realm. It's crazy for us as a race to not leverage the potential of what is possible!

Take The Lead

What would it take for traditional leadership training to embrace full reintegration as a core philosophy?

I often remind leaders that they lead human beings, and what comes with the human territory are certain dynamics that harm the potential of what is possible – individually and collectively.

As a self-confessed "crazy one" and "nutter," I see great disconnection in current leadership practice. It comes from resistance to trusting the unknown realm and resistance to understanding integrally what it means to lead co-creatively.

Can you imagine traditional leadership providers embracing awareness-based training education to evolve leaders to higher levels of awareness, capacity, and operation?

If I can survive and transcend the most horrific experiences a human being could ever face in this lifetime, then anybody can attain transformative change to the level of transcendence.

We have some new world problems on our doorstep and new ones coming we have not even experienced yet, so there is a sense of urgency to evolve the consciousness of those who lead for we will not be able to solve these problems by using the current level of thinking within the traditional leadership approach, as quoted by Albert Einstein.

Recommendation

I will leave Steve Harvey to close this chapter with his phenomenally inspiring video "You Have to Jump":

https://www.youtube.com/watch?v=-PdjNJz7B1Q

4

LEVERAGING
INDIGENOUS WISDOM

Spirituality is not new. It's thousands of years and hundreds of generations old, and we have a lot to learn from this ancient wisdom.

I have always been fascinated by cultures and cultural perspectives, because they embody what it truly means to trust the unknown realm.

In this chapter, we'll explore some of this indigenous wisdom and learn what it can teach us about co-creative leadership.

Some who read this chapter may discount it as old and primitive – like "Stone Age thinking in a high-tech world."

The default identity I spoke about in the previous chapter will automatically discount or dismiss anything that's uncomfortable, unsafe or unknown. That's OK. Bear with me!

The business world is chronically spiritually bereft! If the soul of each individual human being in business is fragmented, then the collective whole of our business infrastructure globally is also fragmented.

We would not even be here today if we didn't leverage the learnings from indigenous cultures. I am bold enough to say that I believe the business world has a lot to learn from the wisdom of the ages.

So let's take a brief look at ten different cultures, their views on faith and spirituality, and what it means to them. You'll see how they view the power of the spiritual element being an integral part of the human existence and the evolution of the human race.

Māori Culture

The origin of Māori has been reliably traced to the islands of Eastern Polynesia, and their journey to New Zealand occurred in a number of epic waka (canoe) voyages over a significant period of time. These journeys established Māori as daring and resourceful adventurers, and as one of the greatest navigating peoples of all time.

Māori have similar beliefs to many other indigenous peoples. In the time of our grandparents, they had a deep understanding of our natural environment. They knew when to grow vegetables, pick certain berries, fish, and gather seafood.

Since the migration into the cities in search of work, the Māori people took their beliefs and culture with them. Māori led the way for other tangata whenua, people of the land, around the world.

Some fundamental Māori concepts include:

- **Whakapapa** – genealogical descent, lineage

- **Mauri** – the life force, the essence of being, an energy which permeates through all living things

- **Tikanga** – customs, rules, regulations, and protocols

The Māori view of the world can be broadly defined as a series of states or dimensions:

- The material or physical state, which is familiar to most people. It is exposed to us through our senses, and it is the one we can directly observe and describe (taha tinana).

- The mental or intellectual state, which requires us to think holistically to understand the whole system, with all processes, not just one part of it (taha hinengaro).

- The spiritual state, which many people are unfamiliar with. It is the spiritual dimension of Māori culture (taha wairua).

- The related/associative state, which is learned over a long period of co-existence and association with the environment.

  Land, water, and air to Māori are special taonga (treasures). Their use and management require special care and attention.

Native American Culture

The Native Americans lived in separate tribes across the vast continent of North America, and yet many of them shared the same beliefs and culture.

Their religion and traditions are based on the culture of animism, which is based on the belief that the universe and all natural objects in it have souls or spirits. They believe that natural phenomena possess minds, and spirits control the sun, rain, and other forces.

Inuit Culture

The Inuit also believe that all things have a spirit or soul, just like humans – so killing an animal is like killing a human. These spirits are part of the larger environment – the air and sky – and part of the larger whole.

The Inuit believe humans consist of three spiritual parts:

- life force

- personal spirit

- soul

  The life force departs after death, but the other two components can be reborn.

Australian Aboriginal Culture

The Australian Aboriginal indigenous peoples have many different cultures, grouped around tribes and languages.

A new genomic study has revealed that Aboriginal Australians are the oldest known civilization on Earth, with ancestries stretching back roughly 75,000 years.

They have a rich culture involving a custom, lore, and value system based on the sustainability of their spiritual connection, belonging, obligation, and responsibility to care for their land, their people, and their environment.

The six values they adhere by are Spirit and Integrity, Cultural continuity, Equity, Reciprocity, Respect, and Responsibility.

Their belief system incorporates practices and ceremonies centered on a belief in the Dreamtime, where dreaming brought creation into existence. Their traditional healers, Ngangkari, are highly respected men and women who act as healers and doctors, and are custodians of important Dreamtime stories.

Indian Culture

India has one of the oldest civilizations, with an amalgamation of several varied cultures, spanning the Indian subcontinent and shaped over several millennia.

Hinduism is the dominant religion in India, with the core themes of:

- Dharma (ethics and duties)

- Samsara (continuing cycle of birth, life, death, and rebirth)

- Karma (action, intent, and consequences)

- Moksha (liberation from samsara or liberation in this life)

- Yogas (paths or practices).

Papua New Guinean Culture

The culture of Papua New Guinea is many-sided and complex. The population of 7 million has as many as 7,000 different cultural groups, most with their own language.

In traditional Papuan religions, supernatural beings include ancestral spirits and spirits of nonhuman origin, and play a significant role in the lives of Melanesians. Papuans believe that spirits continue to influence the way people act and behave.

African Culture

Culture in Africa is varied and manifold, consisting of a mixture of tribes, each with unique characteristics.

Traditional beliefs and practices of African people include belief in a supreme creator, use of magic, and traditional medicine. Humanity's role is to harmonize nature with the supernatural.

Most African religions believe in a dualistic concept of a person – that is, both body and spirit. Most African cultures have elaborate mythologies that explain the origins of the world.

Chinese Culture

The Chinese culture is one of the oldest in the world, with thousands of years of customs and traditions varying between provinces, cities and towns.

Chinese religion originated with worshiping the supreme god Shang Di during the Shia and Shang dynasties, with the king and diviners acting as priests using oracle bones. Most Chinese people believe that a spiritual world exists, and call on the spirits to answer questions, heal sickness, and provide guidance.

Japanese Culture

Japan is an extremely homogeneous society, but regional variation in social and cultural patterns have always been significant. Most Japanese people place a high priority on pride of people and identification with a particular place.

Ikigai is a Japanese concept that means your 'reason for being. ' 'Iki' in Japanese means 'life,' and 'gai' describes value or worth. Your ikigai is your life purpose or your bliss. It's what brings you joy and inspires you to get out of bed every day. If you have not explored the concept of Ikigai within your leadership development, I highly recommend you do so.

They use the term Shinto to refer to gods and belief in the relationship between people, the natural environment, and the state. The religion has no dogma or scriptures, and Shinto has coexisted with Buddhism, and each has influenced the other.

Zulu Culture

Although most Zulu people now state their religion as Christianity, many also retain their old belief system of ancestor worship – even sometimes in parallel with their Christian beliefs.

The Zulu recognize three components in a human being: the physical body, the life force, and the "shadow" (personality). When the life force leaves the body at death, the "shadow" can live on, but only if the person met certain conditions in life – including respect and generosity towards others.

Are we to deny indigenous wisdom because is it not understood or respected by the majority of Westerners? Why not leverage all the wisdom available to us for the benefit of evolving the consciousness of those who lead and the human species as we know it

Key Learning

This Australian Aboriginal proverb says it all:

"We are all visitors to this time, this place. We are just passing through.
Our purpose here is to observe, to learn, to grow, to love, and then we return home."

5

THE
CO-CREATIVE
AGE

H umanity has gone through a series of transformations over the centuries. We are in the Information Age now, and I believe the next is the Co-Creative Age. What does that mean for you as a leader and for us as a race?

If you look at just the last century, we have been through many periods of transformation:

From	To	Name
1880	1945	Machine Age
1914	1918	World War I
1920	1929	Roaring Twenties
1929	1939	Great Depression
1939	1945	World War II
1945	now	Atomic Age
1945	1989	Cold War
1950	1953	Korean War
1955	1975	Vietnam War
1957	now	Space Age
1970	now	Information Age
2001	now	War on Terrorism
2001	now	War in Afghanistan
2003	2011	War in Iraq
2004	now	Social Age

Some of these periods represent advances in thinking, but how sad that so many of them are defined by war, conflict, and disconnectedness!

If we believe it is possible that the next age is the Co-Creative Age, that is significant because it's not defined by technology, conflict, or social change. Instead, it's an age of a new kind of consciousness that is sorely needed for our evolution as a species.

Go Beyond The 3 Dimensions

Most leaders operate in what I call 1-to-3 dimensional space. They live in the realm of meaning, and meaning creates suffering. All human suffering is a function of what we make things mean.

When you evolve beyond meaning into the realm of equanimity (which we will cover in detail in a later chapter), you move beyond the first three dimensions – and beyond meaning, suffering and adversity. You operate at a higher level of consciousness, where you can be the observer, detached from man-made meaning.

In my first book, *'Freefall – Living Life Beyond The Edge'*, I talk of a concept called "culturalization," where you no longer need to create adversity to learn because you're operating at a higher level of consciousness. Currently, the only way we evolve as a species in our current level of consciousness is through the need to manifest adversity to learn. Imagine a world where we could evolve beyond the need to suffer as a race.

I strongly believe there is a need to evolve current leadership teachings to that of the 4th/5th dimensions and beyond – beyond the realm of physical reality.

Evolve To Alchemical Intelligence

In the business world, leaders talk about analytic intelligence, or IQ, which is all about thought and the individual. This has been the dominant kind of intelligence in the business world, and indeed in the educational system as well.

Many now embrace emotional intelligence (EQ), which is about emotional freedom and beginning to open to others. A few even accept (or at least tolerate) spiritual intelligence (SQ), which starts looking at wisdom and a higher purpose.

These intelligences – IQ, EQ, and SQ – lay the foundation for higher levels of intelligence: holistic intelligence (HQ) and alchemical intelligence (AQ).

Here's a summary:

LOCATION	CONNECTION	INTELLIGENCE	UNDERSTANDING
MIND	Individual	Analytical (IQ)	Thought
HEART	Beginning to open to others	Emotional (EQ)	Emotional Freedom
SPIRIT	Higher purpose / Self	Spiritual (SQ)	Wisdom
SOUL	Connecting profoundly to others / collective consciousness	Holistic (HQ)	Knowing
ALL	Connecting to all you can be and will be	Alchemical (AQ)	Evolution

Alchemical intelligence is about operating from potential – your own potential and the potential of others. Ultimately, it's also about the potential of your community, organization, nation, the world, and the legacy you create for the future.

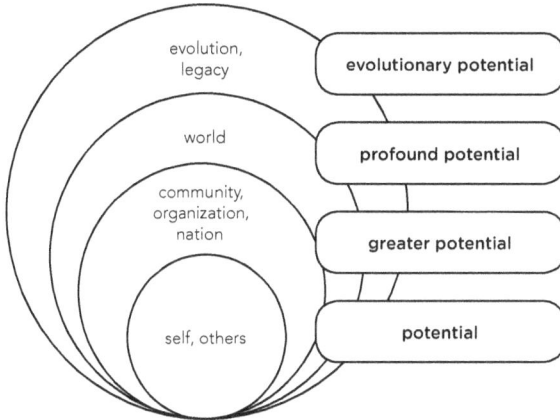

When you operate in the space of IQ, EQ and even SQ, you operate at the mind, heart, and spirit level. You tap into potential at the self, other, community, organization, and nation level. When you operate at the higher consciousness of HQ and AQ, you operate at the soul and "all" level, and tap into profound potential and evolutionary potential.

Abraham Maslow touched on this in his famous "Hierarchy of Needs." He says we can't operate at higher levels until we have our needs met at lower levels. For our conversation here, the most important point is his highest level: self-actualization. This is the level of alchemical intelligence, where you create profound and evolutionary changes.

There are very few people walking the planet who are self-actualized, and that's a waste of human potential. It means that too many members of the human race are failing to realise their highest potential in their human existence.

The very act of "being human" should be a journey to experience self-actualization and be integral to evolving the consciousness of those who lead!

The God Spot In The Brain/Neurotheology

University of Missouri researchers state the following:

"We have found a neuropsychological basis for spirituality, but it's not isolated to one specific area of the brain. ... Certain parts of the brain play more predominant roles, but they all work together to facilitate individuals' spiritual experiences."

So yes, the potential is there in our brains to develop what is termed the "God Spot" or "God Zone." However, most people don't use it to its full potential.

I once worked with a neuroscience researcher who, together with leading researchers in some of the top universities around the world, had developed a profile to assess the "God Zone." When I completed the profile, he said he was shocked because he had never seen a profile like mine – with the "God Zone" the largest he had ever seen. I was intrigued to say the least.

An emerging field of research, neurotheology, also known as spiritual neuroscience, attempts to explain spiritual experience and behavior in neuroscientific terms. It is the study of correlations of neural phenomena with subjective experiences of spirituality and hypotheses to explain these phenomena.

For more, watch these videos:

- "Neurotheology: God is in The Neurons," which is the first chapter of the documentary "Athene's Theory of Everything", and covers the research of Chiren Boumaaza ("Athene") in 2010.

- Morgan Freeman's thought-provoking documentary series "The Story Of God".

My point is that there's a lot we don't know and don't understand, but that doesn't mean it doesn't exist. I believe strongly that educating leaders to evolve their consciousness is mission critical, and currently this is sadly missing in traditional leadership teachings.

Key Learning

Who you are in your human form is limited, yet who you are in your co-creative form is limitless. If this is the case, why on Earth is exploration of unknown dimensions not embraced within leadership development?

Pre-Covid, the leadership landscape was very traditional, linear, masculine focused on hard skills. Post-Covid, the entire leadership landscape has changed, embracing new approaches to leadership, those that are more oriented to nontraditional, nonlinear, soft skills (or as I would prefer to term 'human skills'). Leaders are used to being in control; post-Covid they were thrown into uncertainty to unprecedented levels. That being the case, we cannot but not change how we lead and that requires evolving the consciousness of those who lead to learn how to navigate the terrain of uncertainty. Current leadership practices will not address the new world problems on our doorstep or those that haven't even occurred yet.

What are you currently doing to evolve your current consciousness in how you lead? What changes are you embracing for yourself and your people?

Thank you for staying with me so far on this journey. But you might still be wondering:

"What relevance does this have to me?"

"What's in it for me?"

"Why should I bother?"

"Why should I listen?"

These are good questions and my aim is to answer them here.

If you're championing an important cause – like reducing teen suicide, or ending child trafficking and the like, you do not need these answers because you are already connected and associated. Sadly, a high percentage of the 8.1 billion people on the planet are disconnected.

If we're disconnected and disassociated, it's easy to disconnect and dissociate from what's happening around us, whether it's cruelty to animals, starving children in Ethiopia, or any of the many other issues we face today.

Your Human Existence Makes A Difference

Any significant change hasn't happened because of the masses, but by one, two, or a few committed people who have been able to impact the masses. As American anthropologist Margaret Mead was quoted as saying:

"Never doubt that a small group of thoughtful, committed people can change the world. Indeed, it is the only thing that ever has."

There are people out there who need you. While you're making do at a lower level of consciousness because of your default identity, you're not contributing to the groundswell of what could occur on the planet.

When you awaken to the legacy of why you are here, you directly impact future generations who aren't even born yet. We all have a responsibility to awaken and evolve. I often say to my clients, who I have the privilege to work with, "I am not directly interested in just 'your transformation,' I am interested in the lives you are yet to transform when you get out of the way!"

Why the urgency? Take climate change as a good example of how disassociated we are as a human race. We, as a society of humans, disrespect Mother Earth, FACT. We live as though planet earth can sustain the harm we are constantly inflicting on it. Thinking about, talking about what we need to do **will not** address the critically important issues facing our planet.

Yes, I'm Talking To *You!*

You might ask, "Why should I care? who am I to change the world," and my response usually is, "Who are you not?" We are all being called whether we wish to acknowledge it or not. If you were to refer back to the 'Hero's Journey,' by Joseph Campbell, you may recall the following phases:

- **They hear the call and deny it.**

- **They hear the call, act on it, but come up against trials and tribulations.**

- **They hear the call and see it through to fruition.**

If you're at the second or third level, you understand the urgency already. You have awakened to a level where you know what's possible. You realize there's no choice but to go on, and you can't (and won't) back out.

However, if you're at the first level, it's not necessarily easy to understand the urgency.

You're operating from your default identity, where everything is to do with safety. It makes sense that you don't trust the unknown, and won't follow the calling because it's not safe to do so.

"It's not safe to step out."

"It's not safe to trust the unknown."

"Look what's happened in the past."

I get it. But we won't evolve as a human race if we remain disassociated and operate out of our fear of evidence that we've found in the past.

So ... What if I could show you that it *is* safe to follow your calling? What if there was a bridge, a formula, and a solution? If I could show you how to take away all the concerns and the reasons for not doing it, will you take that step?

I hope you will, because the costs of *not* doing it are too great.

Right now, it's convenient to stay disassociated and confused, because you don't have to take responsibility. It's too easy to "clock out." That's the function of your default identity.

It might be serving you now to keep operating from the default identity, and maintain the status quo, but it won't stay safe and convenient forever. The impact of not evolving to your highest potential is significant.

We're facing some serious dynamic changes on the planet now, and most of the proposed solutions aren't sustainable.

In the movie *The Matrix*, the hero Neo is given the choice between a blue pill and a red pill. The blue pill returns him to oblivion, living in a fabricated reality. The red pill takes him into the "real world" – in our language, it gives him the chance to embark on the Hero's Journey.

Some people will choose the blue pill. If you're reading this book, I know you're not one of them. Take the red pill.

In summary, let's answer the questions above:

• What relevance does this have to me?

Are you human? It's relevant – you impact the whole!

• What's in it for me?

An unrecognizable life of dimensions you have no concept of.

• Why should I bother?

The cost of not bothering is soul destroying.

• Why should I listen?

We were all born with free will. You indeed have a choice – so what will *you* choose?

Awaken The Sense Of Urgency

In John P Kotters book, A Sense Of Urgency, he writes, "most organizational change initiatives fail spectacularly (at worst) or deliver lukewarm results (at best)." In his international bestseller, Leading Change, John Kotter revealed why change is so hard, and provided an actionable, eight-step process for implementing successful transformations. The book became the change bible for managers worldwide.

Now, in A Sense of Urgency, Kotter shines the spotlight on the crucial first step in his framework: creating a sense of urgency by getting people to actually see and feel the need for change.

Why focus on urgency? He writes, "without it, any change effort is doomed." Kotter reveals the insidious nature of complacency in all its forms and guises.

Recommendation

Watch John Parker's YouTube video entitled: *Leading Change; Establishing A Sense of Urgency* - https://www.youtube.com/watch?v=2Yfrj2Y9lll

7

LEGACY
LEADERSHIP

n the leadership space, when most people think about the word "legacy," they refer to what you leave behind when you die. But your legacy is also about you fulfilling on your legacy during your lifetime.

Legacy is the most profound conversation you can facilitate with a human being on the planet.

What are you doing here? What is your DNA calling you to be in the world? If your entire purpose for being is to follow your calling, and surrender to what you're being called to do, that becomes the legacy of why you're alive.

You are unique, you are great, you have something to offer the planet that no one else can.

When you look at it that way, legacy leadership takes on a whole new purpose.

A Sustainable Legacy

Why do organizations globally – including businesses, governments and others – place so little importance on succession planning?

If we are so evolved as a race, why wouldn't we mandate succession planning as one of the most crucial elements in our evolution?

In most governments around the world, where are the true quality candidates to vote for? Some politicians say succession planning is important to them, but if that was true, we would have more quality candidates. Those voted into power have awesome power and run our countries. Surely this would warrant a sense of urgency for legacy leadership.

Joseph Jaworski says in his book '*Synchronicity : The Inner Path Of Leadership*':

"Defining your leadership legacy is an intentional act that calls us individually to serve those who we lead in a manner that is best for the greater good. A high percentage of leaders are focusing on survival and reinvention, yet they should also be paying attention to their legacy. Not to promote themselves, but to have a positive impact on the whole organization and community. When leaders are connected to something, to each other, this connection immediately allows a higher individual and collective purpose to emerge."

In the organization you lead, are you forecasting 5, 10, or 20 years ahead? What is your succession plan? Who will be the future emerging leaders within your organization?

If you don't make legacy as paramount as Vision and Mission, you are limiting the potential of what is possible. Is your company living its legacy within your culture? If not, why not? If so, when?

This Is *My* Legacy

My vision statement is:

Impacting Future Generations Through The Fulfilment Of Global Legacies

This is not only my vision statement but also my legacy in this lifetime. Birthed in 2010.

It can be articulated as follows:

I BELIEVE THERE WILL BE A DAY WHEN:

- Traditional leadership models evolve beyond the humanistic realm to that of the co-creative realm.

- The coaching industry raises the bar on walking the talk and a level of unprecedented authenticity is manifested in the coaching profession.

- Those called to the profession of coaching embrace "healing" as an integral modality to ensure sustainable transformation of themselves and their clients.

- Those in the counseling and psychotherapeutic professions prioritize being healed themselves before attempting to heal others.

- Coaching, counseling and psychotherapeutic practitioners adopt the principle of going toe-to-toe personally with their clients to unearth the true gold that exists in the rawness of unprecedented authenticity.

- There is no longer a divide between indigenous and mainstream cultures. The topic of spirituality will no longer be awkward and we once again experience a world of connectedness.

- Depression and suicide are no longer experienced or tolerated as aspects of our societies.

- The human psyche no longer experiences the "inner critic," and we experience the intuitive way of being that is our birthright.

- Human consciousness evolves to the level at which fear no longer exists and love is the primary emotion felt.

- Equanimity rules, and wars no longer exist to propel the wheels of monetary gain.

- We as a species take responsibility for how truly powerful we are, and no longer have the need to manifest illnesses to learn our contractual lessons.

- We no longer compete with our fellow human, in business or in our personal lives, and we all learn the art of co-opetition, which is inherently our natural state.

- Those who have the power on this planet – and they know who they are – collaborate beyond their egos to make the difference in the world from which future generations, as yet unborn, will benefit.

- The face of the education system as we know it will evolve, and the future of our education lies in the establishment of co-creative schools and co-creative universities – institutions that champion the human spirit and feed the human soul.

THIS IS MY LEGACY

MY VISION STATEMENT IS:

IMPACTING FUTURE GENERATIONS THROUGH THE FULFILMENT OF GLOBAL LEGACIES.

This is not only my vision statement but also my legacy in this lifetime. Birthed in 2010. It can be articulated as follows:

I BELIEVE THERE WILL BE A DAY WHEN...

Traditional leadership models evolve beyond the humanistic realm to that of the co-creative realm.

The coaching industry raises the bar on walking the talk and a level of unprecedented authenticity is manifested in the coaching profession.

Those called to the profession of coaching embrace "healing" as an integral modality to ensure sustainable transformation of themselves and their clients.

Those in the counseling and psychotherapeutic professions prioritize being healed themselves before attempting to heal others.

Coaching, counseling and psychotherapeutic practitioners adopt the principle of going toe-to-toe personally with their clients to unearth the true gold that exists in the rawness of unprecedented authenticity.

There is no longer a divide between indigenous and mainstream cultures. The topic of spirituality will no longer be awkward and we once again experience a world of connectedness.

Depression and suicide are no longer experienced or tolerated as aspects of our societies.

The human psyche no longer experiences the "inner critic", and we experience the intuitive way of being that is our birthright.

Human consciousness evolves to the level at which fear no longer exists and love is the primary emotion felt.

Equanimity rules, and wars no longer exist to propel the wheels of monetary gain.

We as a species take responsibility for how truly powerful we are, and no longer have the need to manifest illnesses to learn our contractual lessons.

We no longer compete with our fellow man, in business or in our personal lives, and we all learn the art of co-opetition, which is inherently our natural state.

Those who have the power on this planet – and they know who they are – collaborate beyond their egos to make the difference in the world from which future generations, as yet unborn, will benefit.

The face of the education system as we know it will evolve, and the future of our education lies in the establishment of Co-Creative Schools and Co-Creative Universities – institutions that champion the human spirit and feed the human soul.

SALLY ANDERSON
Founder, Co-creative/
Equanimous Leadership

This fuels my existence as I know it. It is bigger than I am.

Sally Anderson alone trying to fulfill on this vision and legacy? Not possible. Sally Anderson co-creatively with those who resonate with this vision? Without a doubt!

Recommendation

Watch "7 Principles of Leaving a Legacy", by Susan Steinbrecher, co-author of '*Heart-Centered Leadership: Lead Well, Live Well*'.

I also highly recommend reading '*Legacy Leadership : The Leader's Guide To Lasting Greatness*', by Jeannine Sandstrom & Lee Smith.

When we are disconnected and disassociated, we compete out of fear – feeding on either past experiences or future-based projections.

Of course, there is healthy, empowered competition. But most competition is neither healthy nor empowered. It comes from fear, and it keeps us disconnected.

You know it when you see it. It's rife within politics, where what could be healthy debate is reduced to name-calling and criticism because of a fear of losing.

You see it in the business context as well. Some organizations are preoccupied with their competitors, out of fear of losing market share. Keeping an eye on the market is healthy; obsessing over it to drive all your decisions out of fear is not.

People operate at that level because of their level of consciousness. Fear is fueled at the level of disconnection and disassociation.

In contrast, if you operate at a higher level of consciousness, you come from an abundance mindset, where you trust there's enough business for all and have a genuine sense of wanting to work with others.

That's co-opetition, a healthy relationship with wanting to collaborate, support, pay forward, and respect mutual goals and aspirations.

Co-opetition Is More Than Just Collaboration

Some businesses gain an advantage by working together with suppliers, customers and other businesses producing related products. That's collaboration, but co-opetition goes further.

At the humanistic level, collaboration is indeed a step up from fear-based competition. At a higher level of consciousness, co-opetition happens at a spiritual level, where you tap into the limitless unknown realm. At that level, you're a co-creative being, tapping into your intuition and being able to trust and access the unknown.

When we were born, intuition was our lifeline to the unknown. Then we became disconnected, and lost the way to tap into that co-creative self. So most people operate from their default identity.

When each person operates from their default, it shapes the collective default within an organization. That has an impact on results, which affects how we function as a society.

On the other hand, if we all realized there is another way, it would transcend our current experience as we know it. What would happen if corporations globally learned the art of co-opetition rather than competition?

Competition is about fear. Co-opetition is about love.

Have you noticed resistance to the word "love" in the business context? I find this fascinating. Every business is made up of human beings, and the core emotion for every human is love. Why then wouldn't love be an integral part of evolving how we lead businesses in the future?

Let's Redefine Co-opetition

- **Co-opetition:** Cooperation between competing companies. Businesses that engage in both competition and cooperation are said to be in *co-opetition*. Certain businesses gain an advantage by using a judicious mixture of cooperation with suppliers, customers and firms producing complementary or related products.

Co-opetition: Cooperating with each other from the premise of love *and* leveraging your connectedness to the unknown realm through the power of your intuitive ability.

Some leaders may find this definition confronting. I am not undermining the power of collaborating with other people, but when you collaborate with the unknown, what you can access is beyond comprehension!

When I work with leaders unfamiliar with this concept, I love seeing them find powerful evidence when they open themselves up to exploring their co-creative ability.

I would love to see this being experienced by the majority, not just the minority. For this to happen, we need to stop resisting the unknown realm.

Think of the amount of energy expended globally on fear about your competitors. Surely this collective energy could be used to create a completely new business paradigm! As part of our 20-year vision and legacy, we at Co-creative Leadership teach the principles of our definition through our awareness-based training curriculum and philosophy.

Recommendation

At TEDxPotomac, Berit Oskey spoke about "Co-opetition: A Brave New Business World." There are elements in this presentation that resonate with the points in this chapter.

https://www.youtube.com/watch?v=ESd_PXz4xGs

At TEDxUCPPorto, Felix Buchbinder made the presentation "Let's teach coopetition business models at school."

https://www.youtube.com/watch?v=o0C7Cwuddn8

EVOLVE THE CONSCIOUSNESS OF THOSE WHO
LEAD, WHO CAN THEN MAKE
THE DIFFERENCE FOR FUTURE GENERATIONS TO
COME

"There is almost a sensual longing for communion with others who have a large vision. The immense fulfillment of the friendship between those engaged in furthering the evolution of consciousness has a quality impossible to describe."

Pierre Teilhard de Chardin

9

DISCOMFORT, RESISTANCE AND CONFRONTATION

Think of a time you coached a reluctant team member to step up into a new role. You could see how this role would help them grow, you could see how it was the next natural step for them, you could see the opportunities it would open up for their career, and most of all you could see their potential.

The problem was: They couldn't see all these things. So you had to gently (and sometimes not so gently) push, prod, and cajole them into it. Even so, it wasn't easy. They were uncomfortable stepping into the role, they resisted it, and perhaps they even fought you about it.

You persisted, because you saw their potential, and knew it was worth them walking across hot coals to achieve it.

Eventually, when they achieved it, they saw it as well. Now that they were on the other side, they understood that the discomfort, resistance, and confrontation were worthwhile. In fact, they were necessary to get to the other side.

How Do You Respond To These Words?

Discomfort. Resistance. Confrontation.

How do you respond to these words?

Usually these emotions are viewed as disempowering, yet they can be very empowering.

Most leaders don't embrace them, yet they are mission critical to their evolution as a leader. If you understand and embrace them, they are the cornerstone to living in the unknown realm and accessing the limitlessness of what is possible.

These three states of discomfort, resistance and confrontation are rarely, if ever, mentioned in leadership. I've attended more leadership training and development programs than most leaders, and it amazes me they never discuss these three states – and yet they are critical in their ability to produce exemplary results.

As with everything else, there are two contexts: the disempowered context and the empowered context:

- From a disempowered context, these states hinder progress and cause fear and uncertainty.

- From the empowered context, they are the exact opposite: opportunities to make progress and signals to sustainability.

This table shows the difference between the two contexts, and summarizes how people approach discomfort, resistance, and confrontation in each.

AREAS	DISEMPOWERED – LIMITED POTENTIAL	EMPOWERED – UNLIMITED POTENTIAL
Communication	Withdraws, lacks self-expression	Courageous, unstoppable
Confrontation	Triggered, withdrawal	Opportunity for change, embraces confrontation
Fear	Hinders performance, fears consequences	Searches for it, lives on the other side of fear
Energy	Overwhelmed, stressed	Sustained energy levels
Output	Limited	Unlimited

AREAS	DISEMPOWERED – LIMITED POTENTIAL	EMPOWERED – UNLIMITED POTENTIAL
Effectiveness	Questionable	Highly effective
Performance	Erratic	Sustained
Meetings	Ineffective	Highly productive
Competition	Operates from scarcity	Operates from abundance
State management	Oscillates between empowerment and disempowerment	Sustains empowered state as a way of being
Vulnerability	Not used to sharing vulnerable nature	Completely and utterly transparent
Focus	Leans towards what is known	Focuses daily on the unknown
Disempowered personality types	Struggles with cynicism, skepticism, controversy	Welcomes cynicism, skepticism, controversy
Faith	Evidence-based, lacks ability to trust	Trusts implicitly

Elite Performance

As leaders, it's our responsibility to transform our relationship with these three states so they become empowering rather than disempowering.

That might sound alien to you, but you see it often in elite sport. Less successful athletes fear these states, perceive them as barriers, and buckle under their pressure. The most successful athletes embrace these states, and use them to stay on the court, because they recognize they are integral to producing results at the top level.

I should point out that I'm not expecting leaders to immediately go out and start confronting people. That would be what the default identity would do: find evidence to discount a possibility. Empowered confrontation provides insight into achieving extraordinary results.

For example, when you wish to back out of a conversation, you lose all connection to a possibility. Yet when you *use* the confrontation as an "access point" to stay in the conversation (when you want to back out, *go in*), you will find new evidence. The millisecond you back out, you miss a golden opportunity to connect and witness transformative results.

Go Looking For These States

Leaders who are committed to evolving to the highest potential go looking to be uncomfortable, go looking to be resistant, and go looking to be confronted. They do it with integrity, pride, and a sense of humor – *but they do it!* That's where true transformation lies.

If you don't transform your relationship with these three states, you can't evolve to experience what's possible on the other side. You will fear and avoid them, and won't go close to the opportunity they offer.

I understand why most people don't like these states. I get it. But I also think it's another convenient excuse for why they don't evolve.

How convenient you're uncomfortable! How convenient you're resistant! How convenient you're confronted! They give people an excuse to let themselves off the hook, get off the court, and not take responsibility. As a leader, it's your responsibility to transcend these three states.

For example, consider the elite tennis player who plays at Wimbledon. When the ball is coming their way at a zillion miles per hour in front of millions of people and they miss the shot, they don't get off the court! They have learned that elite sportsmanship requires them to transcend any disempowered thought structures. They use these feelings to fuel their performance.

I believe more emphasis needs to be adopted in leadership development training on the empowered benefit of confrontation, resistance, and being uncomfortable to produce exemplary results. Every leader is human. Human nature tells us to get off the court when these three states are present. If you want to experience exemplary results sustainably, you need to transform your relationship with these three states.

Recommendation

As a change agent, it is your responsibility to go looking to be confronted, go looking to be resistant, go looking to be uncomfortable for this is where the real gold lies. When you do, it becomes your new comfortable and you find evidence to live there. I highly recommend pushing the boundaries on what is familiar. It astonishes me that there is little written about 'embracing resistance,' like breath. There is a lot written about determination, commitment, integrity, resilience, courage, yet to access these states one must face major resistance!

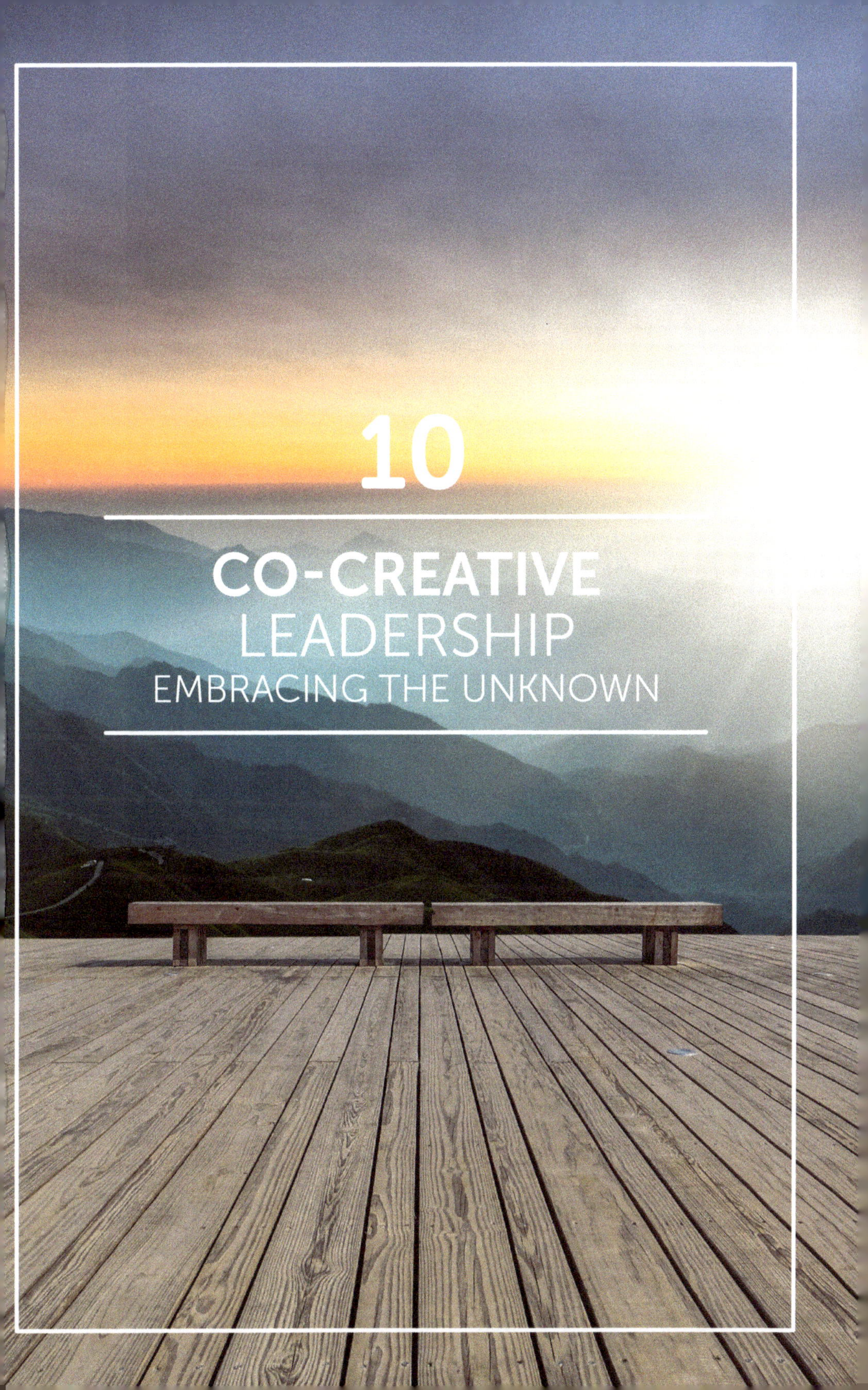

10

CO-CREATIVE LEADERSHIP

EMBRACING THE UNKNOWN

When elite athletes are "in the zone," they say time slows down, reaction times speed up, and they know what to do long before they have to do it.

When was the last time *you* really felt in the zone? When I ask leaders this question, they recall events like:

- making the perfect golf stroke, when everything magically came together at the right time;

- skiing a tricky run perfectly, knowing exactly what to do at every microsecond – that feeling of disappearance, being "at one" with the mountain;

- hammering out a difficult deal, bringing together opposing parties by knowing – almost intuitively – what to say and what not to say at every moment in the negotiation.

Most leaders know what it's like to be in the zone, but don't know how to live there *all the time!*

Most leaders have no comprehension that living in the zone is possible. They only experience a few moments of being in the zone. I am here to tell you it is not only possible but achievable when you learn the art of co-creative leadership.

Co-creative Leaders Trust The Unknown

Co-creation means tapping into the collective consciousness of the universe, working in tandem with it to create unfathomable and previously unthought-of possibilities.

In a co-creative state, you can experience a higher level of engagement, enjoy a oneness of being, and transcend limited humanistic thinking. We term this accessing the 4th/5th dimensions and beyond of leadership.

I return again to the point that who you are in your human form is limited, while who you are in your co-creative form is limitless.

Most leaders have moments of intuitive insight, but they don't live intuitively. I'm not saying they are not effective leaders; only that their current knowledge is limiting their potential. In the co-creative state, you experience a high level of engagement and clarity, which transcends your current humanistic thinking.

I should warn you that because of the default behavior within the human psyche, many people have a massive, vehement resistance to even just exploring this idea.

For example, a past client once said, "I never trust anything that I don't see." That's the automatic response, the scientific angle, the "Prove it to me and then I'll trust it" type of thinking.

If you're thinking this way, it's coming from your 1-to-3 dimensional thinking. This is the realm of meaning, from a high percentage of the human race operates. They attach meaning, which creates suffering, because 1-to-3 dimensional thinking is living at a lower level of consciousness.

The higher levels of consciousness are 4th/5th dimensional thinking and beyond, where you're able to be the detached observer.

Being In Flow!

As a leader, you have responsibility for so many people and accountability for their performance. So the concept of letting go isn't common in traditional leadership teachings. Traditional leadership programs are about leaders having control. In the co-creative realm, the higher power, universal force, or whatever you want to call it, can't access you when you are in control.

Your ability to evolve as a leader is directly proportional to your willingness to be out of control and trust the unknown realm.

Being "out of control" has a very negative connotation – it implies that it is unsafe, unruly, and scary. But I'm not talking about control in that context.

Mihlay Csikszentmihalyi, Distinguished Professor of Psychology and Management at Claremont Graduate University, created the psychological concept of flow, a highly focused mental state that feels like this:

1. Focused concentration

2. Sense of ecstasy

3. Inner clarity

4. Knowing activity is doable

5. Sense of serenity

6. Timelessness

7. Intrinsic motivation

Csikszentmihalyi describes it in his 2004 TED Talk (His presentation skills are not the best, but persevere because he is legendary in the field of flow and leadership):

Many leaders experience moments of flow in other areas of their life, like when spending quality time with their children or playing competitive sport. But when was the last time you felt like that in your leadership role?

To do that, you have to be willing to give up control.

An evolved leader is a conduit, and if a conduit is blocked, then flow is not possible.

I use the concept of vacuuming (I know, I know, most CEOs never vacuum, but bare with me!) and ask, "What's it like vacuuming when you haven't plugged it in and turned it on? Of course it doesn't work!" A high percentage of leaders operate this way!

Being Out Of Control

Leaders are used to being in control (I'm only referring to the disempowered aspect of control here). It's part and parcel of their role. But as a result, some feel frenetic, given the workload they have to manage and the people they need to lead on a daily basis. There is a lot to *do*, resulting in stress, anxiety, and overwhelm.

As a leader, you will access more when you do less thinking and less doing – this is a head-based construct. Leaders tend to lead from their heads as a generalization. To be in flow, one must operate in a connected head and heart space, the result, higher productivity, higher effectiveness, exponential results!

Here are the ten top benefits of learning how to be "out of control" and being in flow as a leader:

1. **Stopping:** When you are out of flow, because you are too much in your head and denying flow, stopping gets you out of your head and back into your heart – the beingness state where you can re-access flow.

2. **Silence:** All answers lie in the silence through your intuition, but to hear the answers you need to silence your mind.

3. **Heightened creativity:** When you are in flow – in the zone – you become highly creative, sometimes to the point where it feels surreal.

4. **Knowing:** When you co-create outside the known realm, you feel 100 percent confident in your own "knowing."

5. **Heightened productivity:** Your productivity goes up because you are co-creating the activity, not just "doing" it. The experience is exhilarating and you can power through and produce better results.

6. **Inspirational:** A leader who has mastered the balance of being in control and being out of control inspires others because they show up differently. They have that "X Factor."

7. **Heightened intuition:** When you leverage your intuitive muscle, it gets stronger and better defined. As a result, you receive more insights, more signs, more direction, and ultimately more energy.

8. **Peace:** A leader who is not solely operating from the thinking mind but also accessing their co-creative ability can access an impenetrable sense of peace.

9. **Belonging:** Being a leader can be a lonely, isolated experience. When you're not controlled by all your mental activity, you return home to your center, which provides you with an indescribable sense of belonging.

10. **Comfort zone:** Many leaders think that what is familiar is their comfort zone, yet we all know it is far from comfortable. The real comfort zone is when you let go and become more integrated in your heart space.

I have often recommended to CEOs that they take half a day off work and, say, go and play golf. Their reaction has been almost like I have murdered their mother! They think if they were to let go of everything they need to *do* in a given week, their world would fall apart!

Sometimes in leadership, you are far more effective when you create the space for new things to come in. Flow can't happen when you're holding on so tight.

Principles Of Co-Creative Leadership

Now let's look at the ten Principles of Co-Creative Leadership.

1. **Embrace confrontation, resistance and discomfort**

Co-creative leadership develops leaders' ability to embrace confrontation, resistance and discomfort as the true "access points" to transformation.

– Sally Anderson

As we discussed earlier, most leaders – and in fact, most human beings – avoid anything too confronting, resistant and uncomfortable. They give up too soon. They stop three feet from the gold, not realizing it is just there if they stayed a bit longer.

A co-creative leader knows they need to go looking to be uncomfortable, resistant, and confronted. That's how they transition from the known world to the unknown world.

I advocate to my clients, 'The minute you want to back out, go in'; that's fearless practice at its best and the basis of 'co-creative leadership'!

2. **Integrate the six realms of intimacy**

Co-creative leadership integrates the six realms of intimacy for the purposes of full reintegration: social intimacy, emotional intimacy, cultural intimacy, physical intimacy, spiritual intimacy, intellectual intimacy. – Sally Anderson

For most leaders, intimacy is a foreign concept – certainly in their role as a leader. Even those who do accept it think of it as authenticity. But it goes far beyond authenticity.

The conversation around intimacy is like Brené Brown talking about vulnerability and shame in the business context. It's a confronting conversation, but one that has now been accepted – and even embraced – by business leaders. Watch her TED Talk online.

This is such an important concept that I devote an entire chapter to it later.

3.   **Embrace skepticism, cynicism, and arrogance**

Co-creative leadership embraces – and even welcomes – skepticism, cynicism, arrogance, and conflict as vantage points for raising consciousness within cultures.

My favorite audiences are those who are skeptical, cynical, and arrogant. They speak out, so I can hear what's going on through their language. Most coaches and facilitators don't welcome this default behavior in their audience, but they are the easiest to transform.

Most leaders shy away from this behavior and these attitudes. But co-creative leaders recognize it's the default identity acting out, and understand why that behavior is playing out. They take it as an opportunity for both parties in the interaction to evolve.

4.   **Leverage the unlimited co-creative realm**

Co-creative leadership transcends traditional leadership methodologies by leveraging the unlimited co-creative realm.

One is limited, the other is limitless. You get to choose which one you access!

10

PRINCIPLES OF

CO-CREATIVE
LEADERSHIP

01

Co-Creative Leadership develops leaders' ability to embrace confrontation, resistance and discomfort as the true "access points" to transformation.

02

Co-Creative Leadership integrates the 6 realms of intimacy for the purposes of full reintegration: social intimacy, emotional intimacy, cultural intimacy, physical intimacy, spiritual intimacy, intellectual intimacy.

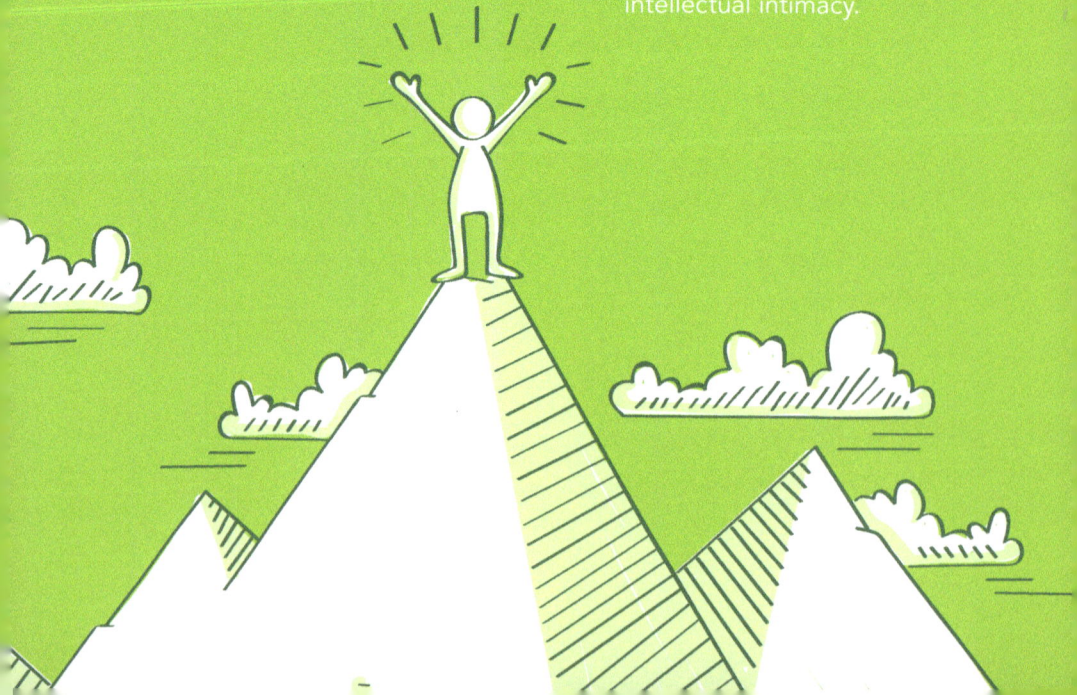

03

Co-Creative Leadership embraces – and even welcomes – skepticism, cynicism, arrogance, and conflict as vantage points for raising consciousness within cultures.

04

Co-Creative Leadership transcends traditional leadership methodologies by leveraging the unlimited co-creative realm.

05

Co-Creative Leadership pioneers raising the consciousness of those who lead.

06

Co-Creative Leadership integrates the 10 Traits of Equanimous Leadership for the purpose of achieving transcendence.

07

Co-Creative Leadership's main operating practice is leading intuitively as the main premise by which to lead.

08

Co-Creative Leadership facilitates conversations most leaders won't have to achieve results most leaders won't get.

09

Co-Creative Leadership operates within the realm of 4th/5th dimensions and beyond, and is not constrained by 1-3 dimensional leadership practice.

10

Co-Creative Leadership is dedicated to the evolution of the human race and teaches sustainable integrated leadership practices.

5. **Raise the consciousness of those who lead**

   Co-creative leadership pioneers raising the consciousness of those who lead.

   I don't want to criticize or diminish traditional leadership, but I do want to point out that it's limited.

   I worked with a new client, who was a high-powered leader in the corporate world. She's a CEO of a multinational company, with responsibility for hundreds of millions of dollars and thousands of jobs.

   I said to her, "If you're as powerful as you are now, even without trusting anything in the unknown realm, just imagine what will happen when we start having you experience the co-creative realm!"

   To most leaders, this is a completely foreign concept. That's not the case across the board, but it's more common than not.

   That doesn't frustrate me; it excites me, because it shows the untapped potential in leaders at all levels.

6. **Integrate equanimous leadership**

   Co-creative leadership integrates the Ten Traits of Equanimous Leadership for the purpose of achieving transcendence.

   Equanimity is the ability to remain undisturbed, to be the observer, and to be able to be with "what is" rather than what you want it to be, could have been, or should have been. It's a key feature of living a co-creative life.

   Again, this is such an important concept that I'll give it an entire chapter later.

7. **Lead intuitively**

Co-creative leadership's main operating practice is leading intuitively as the main premise by which to lead.

Most leaders do not trust their intuition implicitly. And yet, if they surf, ski, play golf, or race motorcars, they know what it means to trust their intuition. They know what it means to "be in the zone" and let go. *That's* being at one with your intuition.

Most leaders trust it every now and then, but they don't trust it implicitly, so they don't flow effortlessly.

Intuition is the biggest muscle in your body, and it's your direct access to the unknown. When you access the unknown at will, you can lead intuitively, all the time, and experience flow consistently and sustainably.

Intuition is such an important concept that we devote an entire chapter to it.

8. **Facilitate conversations most leaders won't**

Co-creative leadership facilitates conversations most leaders won't have to achieve results most leaders won't get.

As a coach, I will have conversations no one else will have, and get results no one else will get, because I'm fearless in my practitioning.

As a co-creative leader, you facilitate these conversations because you know the outcomes from having that level of conversation. These conversations involve naming the elephant in the room. Facilitating these conversations is a skill, because most leaders have a default mechanism that is hindering their performance.

Even high-level leaders have a powerful inner critic that holds them back. Some manage their ability to deal with it, but they haven't mastered it. When you master it, you can facilitate these conversations.

Again, this topic is worth further discussion, and I'll talk about it later.

9. **Operate in 4th/5th dimensional leadership**

Co-creative leadership operates within the realm of the 4th/5th dimensions and beyond, and is not constrained by 1-to-3 dimensional leadership practice.

One realm is limitless and the other limited. One experiences equanimity and the other experiences suffering.

10. **Proclaim sustainable integrated leadership practices**

Co-creative leadership is dedicated to the evolution of the human race and teaches sustainable integrated leadership practices.

Everything about co-creative leadership revolves around sustainability. You are a creative being who can "tap into the national grid." When you're operating in a co-creative fashion, you are never tired and never depleted. Stress and overwhelm no longer affect you, and you have limitless bounds of energy.

Co-Creative Leadership Produces Unfathomable Results

These ten principles show clearly that co-creative leadership is very different from traditional leadership principles and practices.

This table highlights some of the differences.

Traditional Leadership	Co-Creative Leadership
Limited	Limitless
DOING focused	BEING focused
Disconnected	Connected
Control	Empowerment
Authoritative	Inclusive
Inquiry in known realm	Inquiry in unknown realm
Defensive	Collaborative
Manage	Enable
Drive; strive; force	Allow; flow; zone
IQ – Analytical Intelligence	AQ – Alchemical Intelligence
Primarily takes action through thought structures	Primarily takes action through intuitive feeling
Searches for answers from the known realm – through thinking	Accesses answers by being the conduit tapping into the limitless knowledge of the unknown realm

Recommendation

Watch this compelling 45-minute TED Talk by Dr. Alan Watkins, founder and CEO of Complete Coherence Ltd – "How to hack your biology and be in the zone every single day":

https://www.youtube.com/watch?v=0xc3XdOiGGI

Alan is currently an honorary senior lecturer in neuroscience and psychological medicine at Imperial College, London as well as an affiliate professor of leadership at the European School of Management, London. He originally qualified as a physician, and has a first-class degree in psychology and a PhD in immunology.

11

INTUITION – THE MOST POWERFUL MUSCLE

Did you ever hire somebody who seemed all wrong on the outside, but your gut feel told you they were the right person for the job – and you were right? Or perhaps you turned down the candidate who was perfect on paper, but something just felt wrong about them?

Have you ever gone into a deal with misgivings, even though everything looked right on the surface – and then regretted it later? Or did the opposite, and sealed a major deal on a handshake, trusting the other party would do the right thing by you (and they did)?

Even now, you might not know why or how you made these decisions. You might put them down to gut feel or instinct.

I call it intuition.

Intuition Is The Most Powerful Muscle

Most leaders who have children relate to the idea that their kids are connected, fearless, and intuitive. So when I talk to them about being intuitive, they know what it means – yet hardly access it or trust it themselves.

As a leader, you have the potential for great influence simply from your position in the organization. When you operate only from the known realm, your knowledge comes only through study, direct experience, and your culture. That's good, but it's limited. You might have moments of intuitive insight, but they are rare.

When you operate from the unknown realm, you tap into your intuition and are a conduit. You have regular and frequent moments of intuitive insight.

Recall what I said about your moments of flow: When you stand up on the surfboard and ride the perfect wave, take that one golf shot when everything comes together, or ski down the mountain effortlessly. These are the moments of intuitive insight when you're "in the zone."

At those times, you *know* you're operating from the unknown realm, letting your intuition guide you.

When you learn to trust your intuition, you can go a day, a week, a month, a year, and right through to a way of being where intuition leads your life. That's when you reach unconscious competency of living in the co-creative realm.

In the 21st century, we as leaders distrust our intuition and most of us do not realize its power in our evolution as a leader.

Are You Listening To The Static?

When you're listening to your radio in the car and it's not tuned to the right station, you hear static. You don't put up with the static – you quickly tune in to the right station.

There are only four things that disempower a human being:

- Fear

- Inner critic

- Issues, problems and challenges

- Confusion

This is what I term "Human Static".

From the minute human beings get up in the morning to the minute they go to bed, they're listening to the static. They would love to get rid of the static and quickly tune in to the music, but most people don't know what their music is.

Most people don't trust their first thought – their intuition.

In our programs, we teach awareness-based training: the ability to bring to your awareness the degree to which you are disassociated and disconnected. You become aware of your human static, understand why it's there, and learn how to tune in to the music.

We all have a choice. You can live a disconnected, disassociated life in the realm of meaning, continue to suffer, and go to your grave the same way – or you could realize that you have all of the answers through your intuition.

Right now, most people vehemently resist trusting something intangible.

The untrained leader doesn't know how to access the limitlessness of the unknown realm. The trained leader knows the access point is through their intuition.

My life apprenticeship showed me another way. What happened to me in my youth meant I had every right not to trust a goddamn thing on the planet. But it was also the perfect apprenticeship to teach what I teach today.

When you have gone beyond the comprehension of human terror and returned of your own accord, you learn a few things that are not taught in textbooks. I understand what it is to not trust anything, but I also know what it means to trust implicitly. I have the vantage point of both extremes, and I know both realms integrally.

There is a whole new way of living and leading beyond the static that the average human being experiences. I know because I live there every day.

Recommendations

What benefit would you gain as a leader if you were to master your intuitive muscle?

Personal development coach Simone Wright, the author of *First Intelligence: Using the Science and Spirit of Intuition*, describes intuition as "the natural intelligence that allows us to see ahead of the curve, to generate innovative ideas, to communicate powerfully and to do so without having to study spreadsheets or gather piles of data." She goes on to suggest there are seven attributes to intuitive business leaders and they are:

1. They take action based on Vision.

2. They set the trends; they don't follow them.

3. They are able to let go of things that are no longer working or viable.

4. They allow others on their team to thrive, excel, and contribute.

5. They thrive when others tell them, 'it can't be done.'

6. They ask evolved questions.

7. They are able to cultivate solutions and courses of action in multiple directions.

The Spiritual Heart is like a smartphone, invisibly connecting us to a large network. The energy of the heart literally links us to each other. Every person's heart contributes to a "collective field environment." This short video explains the importance of this connection and how we each add to this collective energy field.

12

FEARLESS
LEADERSHIP

I f you have children, you know what it's like to see fearless human beings. They immerse themselves in play, run and jump as fast as they can in sporting activity, and shower their loved ones with as much affection as they can muster.

They really do "dance like there's nobody watching, love like you'll never be hurt, and sing like there's nobody listening," as William Purkey urges us all to do.

This is fearless living, and it's why some toy Superman costumes come with the warning label "CAUTION: Cape does not enable user to fly!"

What about you? When was the last time you were truly fearless? And what if it could be not just a one-off occurrence, but part of a fearless existence?

My number one desire for leaders is for them to lead a fearless existence. I own that and walk that more than most, and I passionately desire all leaders to experience it as well.

Lead A Fearless Existence

When I first started teaching fearless leadership, our brochure and website proudly proclaimed we were teaching "Fearless Leadership," and promised things like, "You will experience the realm of feeling fearless in your ability as a leader."

What I did not realize was that it was a deterrent, not an attraction, because a high percentage of leaders don't want to acknowledge the degree to which fear rules their life, both personally and professionally.

Most leaders don't acknowledge (and don't want to acknowledge) they are fearful. Yet, for humans operating outside the co-creative realm, fear is their most common guide. As a leader, you're expected to be in control all the time and never show fear. But where's the freedom in that?

Even in the coaching profession in some countries, having a coach is viewed as a weakness. It's seen as an indication something is wrong with you rather than an integral strength to your evolution as a leader. I will admit this is changing, but it still has a long way to go. Some leaders view support as a weakness which hinders their ability to grow and expand.

It wasn't always this way. When you were three years old, you *were* fearless. You were intuitive, you were connected, and you felt you could do anything. And then as you learned certain beliefs and behaviors at a young age that curbed your ability to trust the unknown realm, life was no longer safe.

I highly recommend the book *'Stickability: The Power Of Perseverance'*, by Greg S. Reid, as an outstanding and inspirational read. It has countless real-life stories of people who encounter setbacks and obstacles that threaten to derail them from their chosen route. The most successful people adhere to their principles and goals, capitalizing on hidden opportunities even in the face of what many would consider unconquerable obstacles. These people have stickability!

Choose Love Over Fear

At the risk of using another word most leaders don't want to hear, imagine what could be possible if love replaced fear.

There's a fine line between love and fear.

When I coach teenagers, I use the analogy of a train track: The track only has to move a millimeter and the train goes in a completely different direction. It's the same with love and fear; just a minute shift that switches us from fear to love.

There's a whole universe between them, but it's a fine line because all it takes is making a choice through awareness. You make a choice to be connected or disconnected, to be associated or disassociated, and to choose love or fear.

Love is such a difficult subject to discuss in organizations and businesses. I find that hilarious, because every single organization on the planet consists of human beings, who know love, seek love, yearn for love, and experience love. And yet it's not acceptable to talk about it in the business context.

When love replaces fear, it transforms everything. There's just no comparison in what you can accomplish, what you can experience, and what you can feel.

Yet we don't teach it, don't communicate it, and certainly don't encourage conversations about it in the boardroom or the lunch room. Our organizations need to provide more freedom in communication – communication led with love, not fear.

Fearless leadership is the ability to replace fear with love. It means that in every situation, instead of being fearful, ask, "What would love do in this moment?"

That's a very powerful premise from which to operate. I also know it's difficult to accept in the leadership realm, but only because the default identity immediately discounts it.

It Becomes A Self-Fulfilling Prophecy

I'm amazed at the high number of leaders who have either a fear of failure or fear of success (or both). Energetically, it's not surprising these fears lead to sabotage, and they become a self-fulfilling prophecy.

There are some key things to understand about fear:

- Fear is a projection from a disconnected state. When fear is present, you are either out in the future creating a world that has no validity (except the validity you give it) or you are feeding something from the past.

- Fear cannot be present when you are connected and living in the now moment.

- Fear cannot be present when love is present.

- Fear is a barometer of your disconnection from your faith, whatever that is for you, because fear is *not* a spiritual practice!

Fear is rife at the leadership level, and it's not easy for leaders to admit they are fearful. Fearless practitioning is a leader's responsibility. A leader is a change agent. Change agents need to transition not only their own fear, but that of those they lead.

The Cost Of Fearful Leadership Is High

We are supposed to be the most evolved species on the planet, and yet we are still killing each other! We have all this knowledge, all this technology, all this ability to communicate, and yet we're still killing each other. Don't you find that ironic?

A high percentage of businesses are singularly focused on the bottom line and sadly a lot of cultures are fear driven to produce results.

No one in any business is motivated by fear, quite the contrary, they are demotivated, and yet the top-down, stick mentality rules in a lot of cases.

As we discussed earlier when talking about co-opetition rather than competition, why is it such a radical concept to consider and treat others as you would like to be treated? It's not a difficult concept, and yet we seem to be missing the ability to change that dynamic.

Unless we change it, we will never raise the level of consciousness on the planet. When you bring people together, you create a culture. If the individuals in that culture operate from fear because of their own default identity, they create a culture of fear. If they could adopt a culture of love, just imagine what a difference it would make.

We Stand For Fearless Practitioning

Can you imagine those working with the human condition – such as psychiatrists, counsellors, social workers, health practitioners, mental health workers, CEOs, doctors, nurses, thought leaders, and entrepreneurs – having access to a tried and proven education curriculum that teaches "Fearless Practitioning"?

If leading with fear hinders the potential of the results experienced, it makes sense that leading fearlessly produces results that were previously not thought possible.

Part of our vision and legacy is to have this education available to those interested in enhancing the human condition.

Given my background in project, portfolio and program directorship and cultural change, I see three categories of organizations where cultural change is concerned:

- Too fearful to embark on implementing cultural change because they view it as 'all too hard.'

- In the middle of the cultural change process and experiencing difficulties, including cost, but in too far to back out of it in the face of it not working to plan.

- At the end of the cultural change process, and it hasn't worked and definitely hasn't delivered the expected ROI.

This has a huge impact on business culture and its evolution. That's why I have made it my area of expertise, coupled with the education developed within Co-creative Leadership, to partner organizations that wish to become conscious and wish to make a significant difference to the landscape of business and leadership as we know it. But for this to occur they have to transcend their relationship with fear!

Peter Guber says:

"Everybody in business shares one universal problem: To succeed, you have to persuade others to support your vision, dream, or cause."

There are two types of fear: one that empowers you and one that disempowers you.

Empowered, healthy fear is about your safety: for example, don't put your hand in the fire, don't walk down a dark street alone. This instinctive safety mechanism is healthy.

The unhealthy fear is the disempowered context of fear that is rife within business and leadership today. The default disempowered identity claims it's all about "safety," but it's dysfunctional. Unless there is more awareness about this identity in all sectors of society, especially leadership, we will be denied evolving as a race.

Recommendation

Every organization on the planet is a make-up of human beings. Surely the future business blueprint is one based on love, not fear; and connection, not disconnection.

What could you and or your company accomplish if fear were replaced by love?

13

INTIMACY AND LEADERSHIP

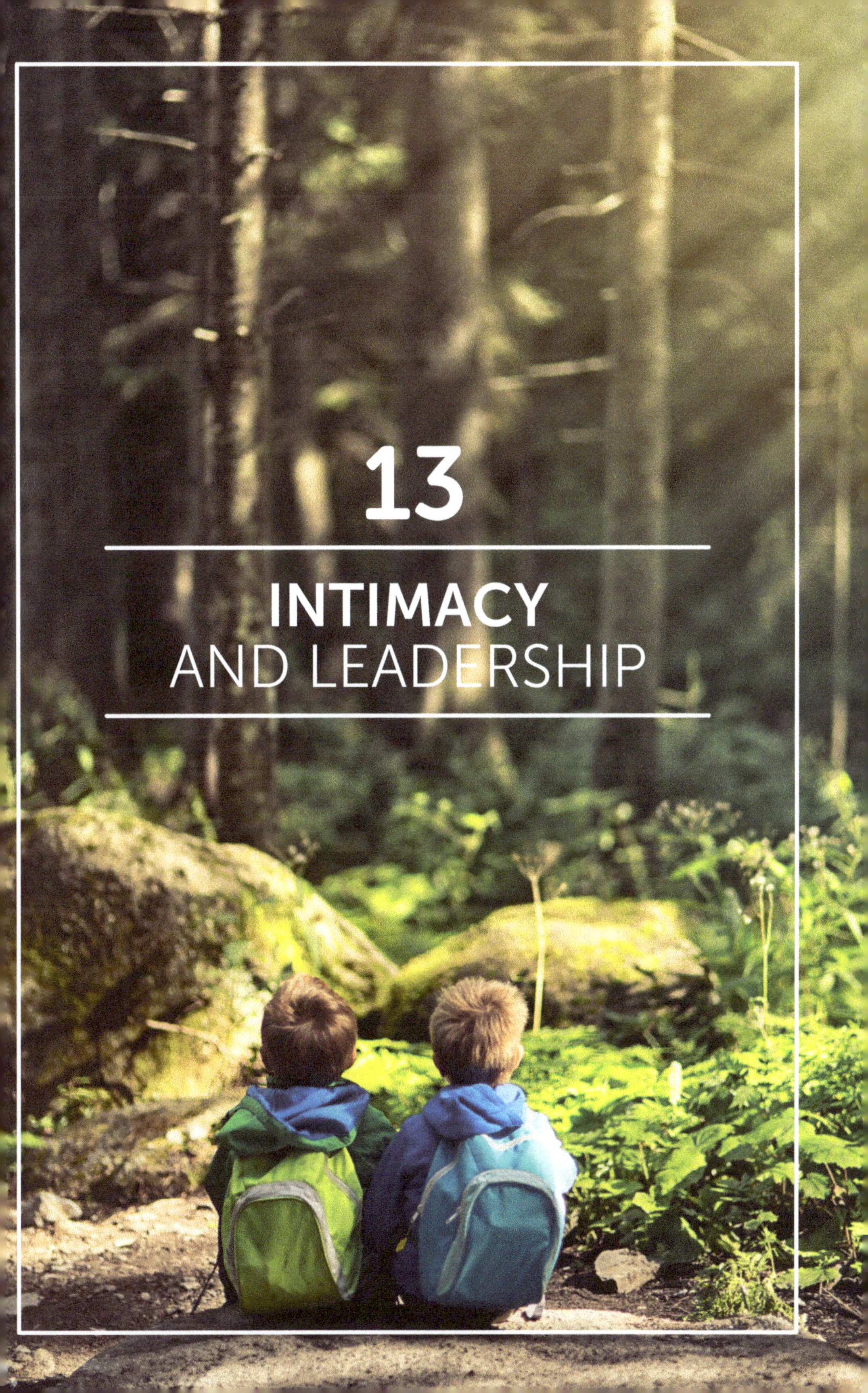

When Brené Brown started a conversation around vulnerability and shame, it resonated worldwide, and she's now one of the most in-demand speakers at Fortune 500 companies. Yet, not so long ago, most leaders shunned these concepts, dismissing them as signs of weakness. Those same leaders now invite her to speak to them and their senior leadership teams – and many take her ideas on board to use in their lives and within their organizations.

It's starting to resonate – even among these resistant, winner-takes-all, spreadsheet-driven CEOs and senior executives – because so many of us genuinely want to evolve and experience a connectedness to something more. They connected to her message because they were human.

The same applies to intimacy.

"Intimate leadership enables leaders to access higher levels of consciousness, thereby expanding their capability to develop mastery of complex demands, which is integral to our intellectual, emotional, physical and spiritual wellbeing."

Sally Anderson

Into Me I See

To me, intimacy is "Into me I see."

To evolve to your highest potential, you need intimacy to re-integrate back into being whole and complete.

Co-creative leadership is all about connection.

In most of the cultural change work I do, one of the most common and fundamental things I find is the degree of disconnection. Much of it comes from not acknowledging the severity or lack of intimacy about what's really happening beneath the surface. That causes severe dysfunction in an organization.

When you are dealing with many people, the more integrated you become in understanding yourself, the more powerful you will be in having compassion and empathy with others.

When you as a leader have more intimate, "open kimono" conversations, you create a very different culture.

A central aspect of the awakening of leaders consists of transcending our fear-based state of consciousness to one of love, intimately connected to all that is.

Why as leaders are we so resistant to exploring modalities beyond the traditional model? This is exactly the space that intimate leadership addresses. But we resist it because it's not accepted as the norm. Unless something is tried and proven, we usually don't favor it, and many leaders don't even want to explore it.

I stand for raising awareness in this area. Go to the places where – until now – you have been unwilling to go.

Integrate The Six Realms Of Leadership

The evolved leadership model has six realms of leadership, each integrated by a different realm of intimacy.

An evolved leader is a:

- **democratic leader** – integrated by social intimacy, which is about vision, unity, and democracy

- **compassionate leader** – integrated by emotional intimacy, which is about communication, empathy, and compassion

- **provocative leader** – integrated by cultural intimacy, which is about wisdom, provocation, and influence

- **intuitive leader** – integrated by physical intimacy, which is about intuition, holistic ecology, and the five + senses

- **collaborative leader** – integrated by intellectual intimacy, which is about performance, awareness, and sustainability

- **co-creative leader** – integrated by spiritual intimacy, which is about connection, legacy, and service.

What's Love Got To Do With It?

Intimate leadership is different from other leadership concepts because of its unique focus on love and intimacy.

You might ask "What's love got to do with it?" What relevance do love and intimacy have in leadership – especially in a business context?

The answer is simple: *Everything!* Organizations are made up of humans, and full of human-to-human interaction. Show me a human being in any environment who doesn't want to be loved, doesn't want to be listened to as great, or doesn't want to be heard.

The leaders who embrace these qualities stand out within their own culture. And if you have a collective of people operating at that level, watch out!

Fear Cannot Be Present When Love Is Present

What could leaders or organizations accomplish if they were fearless? When love and intimacy are present in leadership, fear is not.

But there's a big difference between grasping this at an intellectual level and grasping it at an experiential level. You can say, "That's nice, Sally," but it's not until you experience it that you realize its power.

How many people in your life do you know who consistently and sustainably come from love and contribution? If that happened in governments, boardrooms, and other organizations, our world would be a very different place.

This Goes Beyond Authentic Leadership

You will find a number of leadership programs teaching "authentic leadership." Authentic leadership has been adopted and accepted into traditional leadership training, but is sometimes (although not always) bandied about as marketing hype. I acknowledge and commend the work that has been done in the area of authentic leadership. However, even when applied sincerely, authentic leadership is not enough. Somebody can be authentic, but still not deal with their dysfunction, disassociation, and disconnection.

Intimate leadership goes further, because it includes integration, which explores all facets of knowing yourself, and thus being whole and complete. You experience a connection that is rare in a business context, and you're willing to speak into the space human beings usually avoid.

That said, it terrifies the bejesus out of people, because it's the unknown!

A case in point would be the reader of this book who believes it is important to compartmentalize their world and ensure they keep their personal life separate from their business life. Where you operate in your personal life has a huge impact on how you operate in business. If you are to lead intimately, the two cannot be separate.

The Gold Lies In What Is *Not* Being Said

In all organizational environments, where humans interact with each other, there are many things being experienced but never spoken. The real gold lies in what's *not* being said.

If meetings opened up and people were given permission to speak into the space, in an empowered way, with no judgment or criticism, we would:

- have far more productive meetings, because we would be dealing with reality rather than assumptions;

- experience a very different culture of inclusion;

- have a heightened level of enjoyment and satisfaction for being an integral part of the team – because we feel our contribution is valued;

- value debate as healthy, not detrimental or something to be avoided;

- get very different results.

The Ripple Effect Is Obvious

Multiply this by the number of management employees in the organization, and the ripple effect is huge. With this newfound knowledge, you can propel your organization to better, more sustainable results.

The more conscious an organization becomes, the more they embrace doing things differently and getting a different result. The outcome is evident.

Leaders with an integrated approach to growth and leadership don't experience a disconnect from who they are and what they know. The way you lead growth in one area of life affects all others, because when you start trusting the unknown in the business context, it can't but have a flow-on or ripple effect in your personal life. You transform the relationships with your children, your wife or husband, and your friends and family.

When leaders are connected to something and to each other, these connections immediately allow a higher individual purpose and collective purpose to emerge.

What do you think could be possible if you no longer resisted trusting the unknown realm?

I will close this chapter with a case study where a high-profile leader attended one of our Co-creative Three-Day Leadership retreats while his colleague attended a conference at Yale. They agreed to compare notes after they returned.

When the leader shared his experience at the retreat, his colleague responded, "You are a brave man! I know I could not look at myself to that degree. At least at Yale, I was part of a much larger group. I don't think I could have looked at myself at such an integral level."

I had to laugh; our retreats only take ten leaders at a time for the purposes of personalised attention. You cannot hide in a retreat with ten leaders. Why would you want to considering what you can access? A high percentage of leaders shy away from looking at themselves to this degree, and personally, this has to change!

Key Learning

Consider the six realms of intimacy in leadership: cultural intimacy, social intimacy, emotional intimacy, physical intimacy, intellectual intimacy, and spiritual intimacy.

In each of these areas, how would you rate your current connection to self and your leadership ability?

14

FISH STINKS FROM
THE HEAD DOWN

T his chapter is not meant to offend. Often in the corporate world I was viewed as controversial because I questioned the status quo. My intent was not to be controversial; I just cared about the culture and was willing to honor what I knew was right and just.

The purpose of this chapter is to bring focus to something that is not spoken about enough in traditional leadership. If I am judged because I care about effective, sustainable culture change, then so be it. My stand for this subject is greater than any external viewpoint.

Have you ever worked for an organization that was successful, thriving, and empowering – but the leader was arrogant, controlling, and belittling? Of course not!

I have worked for many years as a business consultant, being paid very good money to work in change programs that cost millions of dollars to implement. But so many of those costly change programs were focused on the dysfunction the head of the organization believed was evident in the culture, but wasn't willing to admit in himself or herself.

I don't want to insult or belittle senior managers and leaders in any way. However, the mindset of the head of the organization *must* champion the change process for it to be effective and sustainable in the long term. It must be led from the top down!

Walk Your Talk

More leaders need to walk their talk rather than just talking their talk. If the head of the organization is not evolving, their people are not evolving either. As a leader, you need to lead this charge. If you want to change the minds and hearts of the people you lead, be prepared to change yours as well.

I can't count the number of times I have been asked to come into organizations as a cultural change agent with the directive to "Fix my people."

I always say sustainable change is *not* possible unless the leader of the organization changes. Only after that happens does change filter down to the rest of the organization.

Sadly, few leaders are prepared to look critically at themselves to that degree, and yet they expect it of their people. A leader who does not remain the student will never evolve in their leadership capability. And a leader who is unwilling to be vulnerable in front of their people is not evolving in their leadership capacity.

Get Off Your Pedestal

There's a degree of arrogance in many high-level leaders. They don't look at themselves as students because they think they know it all – or at least, know more than the people they lead. I believe if you are still here breathing, you are still here learning.

As a leader, you can choose to have a hierarchy or not. People automatically assume a hierarchy, and many people will automatically put you on a pedestal. Choose whether you allow this or not – it's your choice.

In my own business over the years, I do not advocate for having a hierarchy. I never asked them to put me on a pedestal, so I quickly dismantled that construct.

From the minute I wake up in the morning to the minute I go to bed, I'm not interested in what I know. I'm interested in what I *don't* know. For me to stay in the co-creative realm and continue to evolve, I must stay the student.

You are my peer. You have something I don't know; I have something you don't know. Let's co-create together, but on an equal footing.

Hierarchy Creates Distance

When you operate from a hierarchy – whether you create it or assume one is already in place – you distance yourself from your people.

The way you are perceived dramatically influences your team's performance. If you want to get more from your people, have more effective teams, and produce better results for your organization, change how you are perceived within your organization.

Ego gets a bad rap. To be an effective leader, you need a good dose of ego. However, disempowered ego destroys the ability to truly connect with your people. Empowered ego is an integral asset for highly leveraged leadership.

Take Responsibility For Change

As a leader, you're a change agent. It's your responsibility to embrace change, not resist it.

The worst are the organizations with entrenched cultures and entrenched people. The leaders have been there for a long time, the culture hasn't changed, and nobody at that level is willing to change.

If you see dysfunction in your team, take responsibility for it. I know you did not sign up to be a counsellor or therapist, but at a certain level, supporting your people in whatever way is required is part and parcel of your role. EVERYONE in your team is responsible for the effectiveness of its culture.

That doesn't mean you have the right to berate, intimidate, or belittle people. The best leaders operate from a position of equanimity and create a culture of respect. Be open, listen, reflect, respond, and guide – and you'll shift the culture in your team.

A strong culture spreads like wildfire to the rest of the organization – but so does a poor, dysfunctional culture.

For many years I was charged with implementing cultural change programs and I loved what I did, I cared about the people, and I cared about the culture. But in a high percentage of these organizations, the executive would not embrace the same level or depth of change within themselves. As a result, change was not sustainable.

This is why my own organisation, Co-creative Leadership was born. It's a global leadership service provider focused on evolving the consciousness of those who lead at the highest level for the purposes of administering 'sustainable transformation,' personally and professionally.

Recommendation

If you are interested in sustainable cultural change, the leader of the organization *must* be willing to change as much as their people.

15

POWER - POWER
BASED CULTURES

Think about the last time you asked somebody for advice about something important – outside your workplace. It might have been a conversation with your spouse or partner, a chat at the ninteenth hole with your golfing buddy, a phone conversation with an old mentor, or a lunch with an old school friend you still keep in touch with.

Because it was with somebody you trusted, you were willing to let down your guard, share your concerns, and talk about your feelings.

It might have been an emotional topic for you, so the other person would have given you space to speak, vent, and complain. But they would have also stopped you after a while, and turned the conversation around to resolving the issue.

At the end of the conversation, you would have left feeling better, more settled, and more empowered. You might not even have resolved the issue you asked about, but you would feel better able to deal with it.

That's what happens in a power–power interaction.

Organizational Interactions Rarely Work This Way

Contrast that with conversations, meetings, email exchanges, and endless Zoom calls in your organization. Do most of them operate with the same level of trust, honesty, integrity, and respect?

Organizations are made up of human beings, and a high percentage of those human beings operate from their default identity, undistinguished.

As a result, a lot of interactions in a high percentage of organisations are default–default oriented–made up of disempowered communication.

(As an aside, this is true of most interactions outside work as well. It's rare that you have those conversations I described above with trusted people. But let's focus for now on the organization you lead.)

People who operate from their default are disempowered, and they trigger the default in somebody else, which creates a default–default interaction. This in turn triggers the default in somebody else, and so on.

This creates a collective default culture that hinders the organization from achieving what is possible. This permeates the entire organization and spreads to its customers and the community.

Default–default interactions don't work in teams, they don't work in organizations, and they don't work in any personal or professional relationships. So why do we tolerate a dynamic in our communication that *never* works?

Power–Power Interactions Are Different

In our programs, we teach awareness-based training around power–power based interactions, which are totally different. In a power–power interaction, you stay in your power all the time, regardless of circumstance. You treat others as you would like to be treated, and know how to manage their default behavior as something separate from them.

There's a world of difference between default–default cultures and power–power based cultures.

Imagine what could be possible if we moved from default–default based cultures to power–power based cultures – in organizations, in our societies, and in governments.

Most people don't believe it's possible to remain empowered all the time. But the benefit of a power–power based interaction is that the outcome serves both parties, so it's sustainable. And we've proven it with leaders from all walks of life.

If You Want Freedom, Share The Concern

Imagine a board meeting where everybody was empowered, and everybody was communicating in a way that engendered respect. Issues and conflicts still arise, but the group manages them in a way that respects all parties.

Imagine if equanimity was present in the face of the countless issues facing the organization.

If you want freedom in communication, share the concern. Vulnerability is the access point to shift any human being.

Most leaders don't experience freedom in communication for two reasons: the space is not created for this level of communication and it's fundamentally not safe. There is so much withheld communication in corporate life. A whole new realm of possibility exists when the concept of vulnerability is embraced and freedom in communication is encouraged.

Sharing the concern is a foreign concept not only in business but also for the average human being. Creating a space for the other party to step into creates a whole new realm of possibility. Keep in mind the person you are engaging with is also human. Frame your communication in a way that always "lands" for the recipient. This is a skill, and one I am committed to having in the hands of those who lead.

In power–power based cultures, people have freedom in communication all the time in a sustainable way. They honor all interactions so all parties are left complete.

Build Inspired KPI Cultures

Why on earth do organizations tolerate disempowered KPI cultures, when they could be creating inspired and empowered KPI cultures instead?

The difference is simple but profound: An empowered KPI culture produces results, and a disempowered KPI culture doesn't.

When it comes to meeting KPIs, most organizations operate from pressure, unrealistic expectation, resignation, disassociation, and "making people wrong." No wonder there's so much stress around KPIs!

What would happen if the KPI culture was about inspiration, acknowledgement, empowerment, encouragement, and excitement instead? What would happen if this was the norm in every team, every department, and every organization?

I encourage you to address the cultural dynamic at play with reference to KPIs, especially if they are not being fulfilled. Changing this dynamic will affect everything in your organization.

When it comes to fulfilling KPIs, it shocks me to see the lack of focus on the causal dynamics at play. Why on earth would organizations continue to tolerate disempowerment in this area when it has a direct impact on the bottom line?

What You Complain About Is What You Are More Committed To!

Expending energy complaining about time is ludicrous! Count the number of hours you expend on this complaint and then you will understand what I mean.

I coach leaders not to use the term "time management," and to replace it with "accountability management." Time management causes stress; accountability management produces results.

Too many leaders expend energy complaining about lack of time. Instead, spend that energy feeling empowered by your spoken word in the commitments you make.

When you stop complaining about never having enough time and focus instead on honoring the commitments you have made, your productivity will skyrocket!

There are limited hours in a day, and it's no wonder the busy executive sometimes struggles – with their day-to-day workload, operational accountabilities, assigned projects, zillions of emails sitting in their inbox, and constant unexpected challenges.

In this environment, if you want to be more productive, set precedents and create firm boundaries.

If you want higher productivity – for yourself and your team – transform your relationship with your spoken word. Time management is futile, but accountability management assures guaranteed outcomes, as long as you transform your relationship with your spoken word. Wherever you see the results, that's where your current commitment lies (Ouch!). If you want better results, transform your relationship with what it truly means to be committed!

Do You Have Your Finger On The Pulse?

Do you have your finger on the pulse of your operation and organization in real time? I have conducted many audits in organizations, and real-time visibility has been sadly lacking in most of them.

Managing your investment company-wide is mission critical, and it's vital you have your finger on the pulse of such a diverse portfolio.

Have you even determined the ranking, weighting, and scaling structure linked to the vision of your organization to truly understand the value of your investments? Have you considered the power of project, portfolio and program management in your organization?

Do you currently run an effective issues register within your organization? Do you know every issue facing every department within your organization? If not, why not? How do you expect to transition to where you wish to be if you don't understand and bridge what's in the way?

To experience an empowered culture, you need to unearth how the organization is currently operating.

"Until one is committed there is hesitancy, the chance to draw back, always ineffectiveness.
Concerning all acts of initiative (and creation) there is one elementary truth, the ignorance of which kills countless ideas and splendid plans: that the moment one definitely commits oneself, then Providence moves too."

W.N. Murray, The Scottish Himalayan Expedition

Recommendation

You cannot put a dollar value on living and leading an empowered life and knowing how to sustain it. What value would you place on you and your executives knowing how to sustain feeling empowered, personally or professionally, regardless of circumstance? What difference do you think that would make to your bottom line?

16

BEING LEADERSHIP
vs DOING LEADERSHIP

love Joseph Jaworski's book *'Synchronicity: The Inner Path of Leadership'* because it resonates so much with the ideas here.

Jaworski founded the American Leadership Forum in the BEINGness state of leadership versus DOING leadership, and the book is his true life story of that journey. Early in his path, he doubted himself, wondering, "Who am I to possibly challenge the heads of Fortune 500 companies about changing the whole dynamic of their leadership style?"

Joseph Jaworski is a stunning example of someone who followed what he was being called to do, in the face of his own self-doubt, and accomplished the unimaginable.

Stop Doing And Start Being

Most leaders struggle because they are *doing* leadership. The best leaders thrive because they are *being* leaders.

Leaders who come from a state of "doingness" are disconnected, and often experience life and leadership in these ways:

- Hard

- Struggle

- Stress

- Overwhelm

- Anxiety

- Pressure

- Frustration

- Loss of vitality

- Loss of power

- No freedom

In contrast, leaders who come from a state of "beingness" are connected, and experience life and leadership in these terms:

- Being in "the zone"

- The experience of flow, ease, and peace

- Attracting synchronistic opportunities

- Resonating and manifesting

- Your goals come to you – like a leaf on the river

Many leaders know they are *doing*, but resist *being*.

For example, consider the concept of adopting an "Empty Inbox" policy. Wouldn't this revolutionize your world? Emails are the bane of most executives' lives, but you don't have to tolerate spending your day "doing email."

How Do You Rate?

I've included a table here of 50 comparative examples of doing leadership versus being leadership. Use this as a self-assessment test and diagnosis tool.

Consider each of the 50 examples, and choose either the left- or right-hand side, based on how you rate yourself. This is not black and white, so just assess "Okay, I tend to be more on this side than I am on that side ..."

For each item you identify with on the left-hand side (doing Leadership), you now have an indication of what you could do to get on the other side.

	DOING Leadership (Default, Disconnection)	BEING Leadership (Connection, Presence, Substance, Essence)
1	You desire to serve yourself; you predominantly operate at a "head" level	You desire to serve others, to serve something beyond yourself – a higher purpose; predominantly operate at a "heart" level
2	You're clear on what you are motivated by nor what you are committed to	You are not only clear on what you are motivated by and what you are committed to, but you live from this premise – daily!
3	You struggle with consistently producing high performance results from your teams	You consistently produce high performance results from your teams because you realize the performance of your team is a function of the precedents set by its leaders
4	You tend to get caught up in the day-to-day activity at an operational level	You know to delegate all operational activity and fully utilize the management infrastructure in place
5	You don't focus at a humanitarian nature – you feel incapable of fulfilling a global vision	You have determined your vision for the planet, are present to living your legacy daily, and actively leverage your co-creative ability to manifest it into reality
6	You often engage in DEFAULT–DEFAULT (disempowered) level of conversation and interaction	You only engage in POWER–POWER (empowered) conversations and interactions
7	Listening is swayed by your default behavior	Listening is great all the time and devoid of your default behavior

	DOING Leadership (Default, Disconnection)	BEING Leadership (Connection, Presence, Substance, Essence)
8	You believe that the most important element in running a successful team is the "people"	You believe that the most important element in running a successful team is having the right people on the right bus going in the right direction
9	You frequently feel "lonely at the top", alone in your position, and preoccupied with "making a living"	You realize you are always connected, never experience being alone; present to "creating a life"
10	You provide answers instead of guidance	You rarely answer a question but guides the individual to source their own solution – you build self-reliance
11	You strive; drive for results	You manifest results with ease
12	You experience being disconnected: no freedom; struggle, pressure, anxiety	You experience being connected and supported – in the zone!
13	Not self-compassionate when failing to meet own expectations	Self-compassionate at all times – compassion for humanness
14	You complain there is never enough time and often feel stressed and in overwhelm – low energy levels	You always have time, the feeling of flow is apparent, and you're always able to sustain high energy levels
15	You often live in past and future-based projections and believe that the attainment of goals is the ultimate – attached to an outcome	You revel in the present moment and realize the achievement of goals is just a bonus – detached from the outcome

	DOING Leadership (Default, Disconnection)	BEING Leadership (Connection, Presence, Substance, Essence)
16	You tend to point the finger, relinquishing responsibility to some external person or situation rather than taking self-responsibility	You are prepared to take responsibility at all times
17	You oscillate between being in your power and being triggered, not knowing how to maintain a balanced state of equilibrium	You operate from your power consistently and know how to de-trigger
18	You continue to do, do, do to get things done, and don't trust the letting go process	You create a space and trust – resonate at a different level relevant for producing results
19	You operate from underlying fear, which in turn hinders progress	You understand the construct of fear and do not allow fear to stop you
20	No morning practices applied as a discipline – never fueled	Morning practices applied as a discipline (non-negotiable) – always fueled
21	You never feel balanced with all of life's demands	You embrace the dynamics of life in all its glory!
22	You never take time out of the business, constantly working at the business	You view quality time out of the business as an investment into the effectiveness of the business – e.g. golf, massage, reading, personal appointment with yourself!
23	You constantly live with issues, challenges, and problems	You understand there are never any issues, challenges, and problems – only projections
24	You struggle to relax	You realize the importance of stopping all activity and relaxing at regular intervals

	DOING Leadership (Default, Disconnection)	BEING Leadership (Connection, Presence, Substance, Essence)
25	Hardly ever present, too busy in the mind chatter	Always present, proficient in collapsing all projections
26	You don't see being in integrity, responsible, and committed as freedom, but as a bind, prison, or constraining	Understand integrity, responsibility, and commitment equal freedom, and realize it is a moment by moment choice
27	You don't trust the intuitive process	You trust your intuition 100%
28	You're hesitant to take risks and be spontaneous – mistrust the unknown	You take risks and are spontaneous because you trust the unknown
29	You view a breakdown as a negative	You realize that breakdowns are inevitable in business and that they are always a precursor to a breakthrough!
30	You experience a powerful inner critic (destructive inner voice) and rarely experience much peace of mind	You understand the dynamics of the inner critic, have healed past wounds, and experience a sense of peace as a result
31	You live true to your persona (mask) – looking good, getting it right, having it handled, operating from fear	You live true to your authentic self – true freedom, looking within for the answers
32	You realize what you think creates your reality but are not vigilant in shifting your thought structures, and as a result resonate and attract destructive situations and experiences	You realize what you think creates your reality and are vigilant with retraining your thought structures to be focused on the direction in which you wish to head
33	You rarely acknowledges your achievements	You own and celebrate your greatness!

	DOING Leadership (Default, Disconnection)	BEING Leadership (Connection, Presence, Substance, Essence)
34	You don't like what you see in the mirror	Accept all facets of yourself and like who you see in the mirror
35	You often experience self-sabotage when things start working	You realize self-sabotage served the old identity and kept you safe, but you no longer need to adopt that destructive behavior, given your commitment to your new identity
36	You harbor resentment and struggle with forgiveness	You don't condone certain behavior but can forgive the actions because you realize the only one who loses is the one who cannot forgive
37	You struggle with admitting mistakes	You realize making mistakes is part and parcel of progress and embrace all endeavors. Have no issue in owning and admitting mistakes with your teams
38	You predominantly focus on what isn't working and rarely experience feeling grateful for being alive	You constantly focus on gratitude, prosperity and abundance thinking
39	Financially self-focused	Financially community-focused and contribute philanthropically through tithing a minimum of 10% of income
40	Life seems hard and a struggle	You believe in miracles and expect them
41	You don't realize the importance of integrity with your spoken word – operate within your own version of integrity when it suits	You realize integrity with your spoken word is fundamental to success in any type of leadership position and life itself. Your word is gospel

	DOING Leadership (Default, Disconnection)	BEING Leadership (Connection, Presence, Substance, Essence)
42	You struggle to deal with conflict and confrontation	Calm in the face of conflict and confrontation, and can always resolve the situation through communication that elicits a positive outcome
43	You relinquish responsibility in throwaway default statements such as "I don't know," "I can't," "I've tried," "I don't have enough time, energy, money, etc."	You're aware of your default behavior and take responsibility to shift your state – you are aware you always know the answer
44	You judge without taking responsibility for the part you play in that "judgment"	Stand for true mastery in not judging or condemning because true masters understand that judgment means the ability to master compassion
45	You tend to place the oxygen mask on everyone else and forget about yourself, and as a result feel depleted	Know to put your own oxygen mask on first and foremost in order to be able to fulfil on your commitments
46	You struggle with saying "No" – often feel obliged	You realize saying "No" requires no justification and never feel obliged
47	You experience being serious and significant and at times powerless	You realize that being serious and significant is a function of being a "victim" and choose instead to be in your power!
48	You talk or think a lot about what you want to do but don't do it	You are always in action, advancing the game to win!
49	You label things as right/wrong, good/bad, should/shouldn't, etc.	Add no meaning to situations. No right/wrong, or good/bad, just "what is," devoid of past or future-based projections, and stay in the present
50	You operate from a position of power	You realize "owning your presence" is far more empowering than jostling for a position of power

If you are interested in evolving to your highest potential as a leader, I strongly recommend learning the art of BEING leadership.

Recommendation

The number one book I recommend to *all* leaders I coach is Joseph Jaworski's *'Synchronicity : The Inner Path Of Leadership'*. It's the most powerful read on the topic of BEING Leadership vs DOING Leadership!

liberate

LIBERATE CURRENT CONSCIOUSNESS TO UNFATHOMABLE REALMS TO THEN PAY IT FORWARD, BECAUSE IT'S ALL ABOUT PAYING IT FORWARD!

IT'S THE ULTIMATE PURPOSE OF OUR HUMAN EXISTENCE

"It is up to us to live up to
the legacy that was left for us,
and to leave a legacy that is
worthy of our children and
of future generations."

Christine Gregoire

17

EQUANIMITY
THE ULTIMATE

According to Wikipedia, equanimity is: "a state of psychological stability and composure which is undisturbed by experience of, or exposure to, emotions, pain, or other phenomena that may cause others to lose the balance of their mind."

What relevance does equanimity have in the area of leadership, you may ask? "Everything!" would be my response. Yet it is not taught within the traditional leadership realms. It should be.

Equanimity, like self-actualization, is the ultimate achievement for every human being on the planet. We have a responsibility to evolve to our highest potential in our human existence. Leaders who reach this level of awareness will transform the landscape of leadership for generations to come.

All human suffering is a function of what we make things mean. The significance of adopting teachings of equanimous leadership is to contribute to ending suffering on the planet, permanently!

Ten Traits of an Equanimous Leader

1. Invest In Personal And Professional Development

Has invested in personal and professional development and reached the realm of unconscious competency

When you first learned to drive a car – at the age of, say, 16 – everything felt a bit clunky. But soon you got better, and now you're unconsciously competent: You get in the car now and don't even think about driving it.

It's the same with people who have sustained the ability to remain in an empowered state. They have done the personal development and professional development work and have now become unconsciously competent at it.

It's more than just having done a few courses! They have been in the trenches, looked at themselves, and consciously done the work.

2. Transcend The Realm Of Disempowered Meaning

Is no longer living in the realm of "disempowered meaning" – knowing that no external circumstance can sway their state unless they allow it

Leading equanimously is a powerful skill because there are many situations where it's easy to be disempowered – with work, children, partners, friends, family, and everything else in your environment. When you can step away from assigning meaning to what happens, you operate from an empowered space.

For example, a leader who has reached the level of equanimity no longer experiences stress and overwhelm.

3. Be The Observer

Able to be the observer in every situation and knows what needs to be done from an empowered perspective

Equanimity is the ability to be the observer of what is, without being affected by external circumstances. You can observe it and understand it, but not give it power.

This does not mean that you are disassociated. It just means you have mastered the ability to be an "observer" of "what is" with no reaction.

4. Be Authentic And Vulnerable

Has a comfort-ability factor to be authentic and vulnerable in all situations, both personally and professionally, realizing that these two traits are essential in evolved leadership

Equanimous leaders practice "open kimono" leadership: They are transparent, authentic, and vulnerable. Instead of worrying about looking good, they have complete and utter freedom to be fully self-expressed.

Authenticity and vulnerability are strengths, not weaknesses. The more you can be authentic and vulnerable as a leader, the more people will want to be led by you.

5. Operate With A Deep Sense Of Calm

Operates with a deep sense of calmness, empathy, and even temperament regardless of what is happening in and around them

When you're able to be the observer, you don't allow your human disempowered emotions to cloud your view. You remain calm and empathetic, and lead from an empowered space.

6. View Every Situation As Being "In Perfection"

Can view every situation as being "in perfection" and can always see the higher reason for why x, y, z has occurred

Given the volume of things leaders have to manage on a day-to-day basis, it's not easy to view "what is" as being "in perfection." The key is your belief system. An equanimous leader co-creates and has an innate inner knowing that anything can be transcended if they believe in the unknown.

7. Understand The Co-Creative Realm

Understands the co-creative realm and can access this state at will

Equanimous leaders understand and access the co-creative realm at will. They communicate with the co-creative realm and leverage its power.

This might sound a bit esoteric, but I'm not attached to what you call it, so choose whatever feels right for you. You experience this realm when you've been "in the zone," "in flow," "on fire," or "kicking all the goals."

When this becomes second nature, you won't be passive in accessing that state at will. It's available on demand, and you call on it to leverage it whenever you want it.

This is an unusual concept for most people. As human beings, we're not trained to demand to get our needs met. The co-creative realm is available to you any time you want it. But most people don't call on it. It's like they have won Lotto but haven't collected the winnings!

10

EQUANIMOUS
LEADER

01

Has invested in personal and professional development and reached the realm of unconscious competency.

02

Is no longer living in the realm of "disempowered meaning" – knowing that no external circumstance can sway their state unless they allow it.

03

Able to be the observer in every situation and know what needs to be done from an empowered perspective.

04

Has a comfort-ability factor to be authentic and vulnerable in all situations, both personally and professionally, realizing that these two traits are essential in evolved leadership.

05

Operates with a deep sense of calmness, empathy, and even temperament regardless of what is happening in and around them.

06

Can view every situation as being "in perfection" and can always see the higher reason for why x, y, z has occurred.

07

Understands the co-creative realm and can access this state at will.

08

Is not reluctant to raise the consciousness of their direct reports and is committed to transforming the culture of the organization by emulating what it means to be equanimous
– sets the standard!

09

Always remains the student, and has evolved beyond the realm of ego and territorialism.

10

King and Queen of calling the "Elephant in the Room" – has full freedom of self-expression in every situation and calls it as they see it regardless of the outcome – will always speak into "what's not said."

I ask again, "What's it like vacuuming when you haven't plugged it in to the power source and turned it on?" Of course it's a bit tricky! We as leaders are limited in what we can access when we do not plug into the power source!

8. Raise The Consciousness Of Others

Is not reluctant to raise the consciousness of their direct reports and is committed to transforming the culture of the organization by emulating what it means to be equanimous – sets the standard!

If you want others to follow you, it's up to you to set the standards. When others see you always in your power, and always calm, cool and collected, that can't help but have a ripple effect. Others wish to operate in a similar fashion, and will follow you.

9. Remain A Student

Always remains the student, and has evolved beyond the realm of ego and territorialism

Many leaders have not evolved consciously and still operate at an egotistic level, where there is resistance to continued learning. Equanimous leaders are more focused on learning what they don't know than staying with what they know.

10. Call It As You See It

King and queen of calling the "elephant in the room" – has full freedom of self-expression in every situation and calls it as they see it regardless of the outcome – will always speak into "what's not said"

In most meetings there are many conversations that are not had. It amazes me that there isn't more focus in leadership teachings about how to "speak into what's *not* said." This is the classic "elephant in the room": the thing everybody sees, but nobody dares mention.

I talk to leaders about how "clean" they are, and I am not talking about their hygiene! How clean are you in your communication? Are you prepared to call the elephant in the room? *All* communication is far more effective as a result!

Facilitate Fearless Conversations

Most leaders would probably not acknowledge that they are fearful. So it's tricky to present what is possible if they are unconscious of what's holding them back. Fear comes with the human territory, due to the inability to trust the unknown realm. Fearless practitioning means trusting the unknown implicitly.

The unique education Co-creative Leadership has developed specifically deals with teaching practitioners how to lead fearlessly, and how to facilitate conversations that produce transformative results. If the practitioner has not done the work on themselves, they can't facilitate this level of engagement. We at Co-creative Leadership are committed to this education being in the hands of those committed to enhancing the human condition.

Recommendation

To lead an equanimous life both personally and professionally is the ultimate, because you cannot put a dollar value on stopping people hurting permanently!

18

THE

BIGGEST ADDICTION
ON THE PLANET

I once worked with a group of CEOs on a super yacht. There was more wealth, money, combined in that group than you can imagine!

In one of the live coaching sessions, a CEO said, "Sally, I've achieved everything I wanted in my life. But there's always another thing, and another thing, and another thing. I always get it, but I never have a sense of accomplishment or satisfaction for achieving it."

I asked him how much he acknowledged his achievements, and he said he rarely did. But he went on to say, "When my employees achieve things, I'm the first to acknowledge everyone. So yes, I believe acknowledgement is very important."

I asked, "Well, why is everybody else worth it and you're not?"

When this was highlighted, he wanted to move on, but I said, "No, no, no – we're going to hang out here." And we continued the discussion. During that session, two other CEOs in the group also admitted they had the same experience.

It's a common story. I've worked with millionaires and billionaires who have everything, and yet they're dissatisfied with their life.

This isn't only among millionaires and billionaires, either. I've had the privilege to coach people from all walks of life for many years, and I often see common themes about dissatisfaction.

You might recognize some of these in your own life:

- They say, "This isn't it yet. I'll be happy when I get the house, the boat, the man, the woman, the car, the salary, the children – or when I'm married, debt free, sell my business, retire, or whatever." There is always some future-based destination where they will be happier than they are now.

- When I ask how life is going, many people say, "I'm getting there!" Where is that place called "there"? There is only the now moment – but, sadly, we as a race are hardly ever here.

- We have a tendency to not be grateful for what we have, and focus instead on the deficit. For example, those who don't have money yearn for the day they do, while those who do are terrified of spending it or losing it, or have some other behavioral dynamic at play.

- Many people achieve goals, but don't recognize or acknowledge them. They move on immediately to their next goal, and then wonder why satisfaction always seems elusive!

- Many people resist believing that happiness, fulfillment, empowerment, and satisfaction are their choices. Sometimes it takes a "hit by a Mack truck" experience to wake up and realize it.

- They throw in an addiction to "drama" in their life – so much so that they can't even imagine what a drama-free life would be like.

- They say they dislike, hate, or feel frustrated by their circumstances – for example, weight loss, financial struggle, and dysfunction in relationships – but won't admit they secretly *love* it because it validates their default identity and keeps them "safe."

- A high percentage of people don't believe it is possible to live a life where contentment is the norm, for they are living in their stories!

- Many people live a life where confusion reigns. How convenient that you are confused, because it means you don't have to be responsible. When you are confused, it serves to keep everything in place as is.

There's Only The *Now* Moment

Dissatisfaction goes back to childhood. When people are unaware of their default behavior, which is formed in childhood, they are unaware how much they have a little boy or a little girl running the show.

We are addicted to dissatisfaction because it's a function of the default identity. This identity is created in our formative years and is created for the purpose of keeping us safe, even if it's dysfunctional.

So many personal development books say, "Be careful what you think, your thoughts create your reality." But we're not disciplined or trained in our society to monitor our thoughts.

If we are the creator of our reality and that is a function of the way we think, then why don't we teach the importance of this as a core subject in traditional leadership training?

There Is No "There"

There is no "there"; there's only the *now* moment, but unfortunately we are never here. We live in past and future-based projections which keep us living in a disconnected state.

Can you imagine a world where we are more grateful and satisfied for what we have rather than focus on what we do not?

If you continue to delay your satisfaction to some future-based world, you will always be dissatisfied in your life. If you're a leader, this has huge ramifications.

As the famous author Anonymous said:

"Yesterday is history; tomorrow is a mystery. All we have is the gift of now – that's why it's called the present."

Although this is a cliché, there is a lot to be said for realizing this distinction. But it's one thing to know it, and another to live it.

Dissatisfaction Rules The World

There are 8.1 billion people on the planet and most are disconnected, living in dissatisfaction. This is in large part what fuels the pharmaceutical industry. We as a society endorse drug-taking to keep people disconnected and disassociated.

Where is the logic in this when there is another way?

Recommendation

Watch this video entitled Celebrities on Being Rich But Not Happy + Giving Advice,

https://www.youtube.com/watch?v=MX1hnaco65U

This speaks volumes for not delaying your satisfaction. Who would you be as a leader if you came to the realization that *this is it* and that all the satisfaction in the world lies in your ability to reintegrate and lead a connected existence?

19

EVOLVING THE HUMAN PSYCHE

To evolve the human psyche, we need to evolve not only what we teach in the education (schooling) system, but also what we teach in traditional leadership curriculums.

I acknowledge and commend those innovative countries making fundamental changes to the education system. I also acknowledge the various factions championing the raising of consciousness of those who lead.

However, what frightens me is the lack of urgency.

A prime example of the human psyche is the inner critic. To be human is to have an inner critic. It annihilates human potential, but nobody talks about it.

I can talk to a nine-year-old child with a vicious inner critic. I can then talk to a 49-year-old client with the same intensity of inner critic, except the client has had four decades of listening to this destructive voice – from growing up with it until now. Despite it, they still achieve to a certain level, but what could they be without that internal destructive voice?

Co-creative Leadership is the only organization on the planet that teaches how to *master* the inner critic dialogue. We are not talking about managing it or coordinating around it. We are talking about silencing it for good. Can you imagine if "Mastery of the Inner Critic" was in the mainstream schooling system? It blows my mind that something so fundamentally destructive to the potential of the human spirit is not only *not* discussed but not addressed in our schooling system and our traditional leadership curriculums.

Just imagine what the human psyche could accomplish if the inner critic dialogue did not exist within our culture!

This is only one example of what I believe needs to be core within our curriculums:

- If I told you we had the solution to ending bullying in schools for good, would you listen to the solution?

- If I told you we had the solution to ending depression as we know it, would you want to know how? I would estimate the 80/20 rule applies here: 20 percent of those with depression genuinely have some chemical imbalance where medical intervention is required, but the other 80 percent of those with "depression" have the ability to transcend their current experience in a non–drug-related way.

- If I told you we had the solution to ending pain permanently, would you be intrigued?

- If I told you we knew how to teach people to lead an empowered existence sustainably, would you want to experience this?

  I could go on, but you get the point …

Figure Out Your Passion – Fast!

Over the past two decades, I have interviewed hundreds of teenagers under the age of 18. I ask, "What are you passionate about? What do you want to do when you leave school?" The answer *every time* is "I don't know." The fact that *that* isn't nailed as part of the core curriculum is a major deficiency. Don't you think it is a tragedy that we do not partner our youth in having crystal-clear clarity on where they see themselves in the future well before they reach the age of 18? It's an epidemic in our school system that *most* young people leave school not knowing what they want to do.

I often say to adults, "If you're under the age of 18 and you don't know what you're passionate about, I might let you off the hook. But if you're over the age of 18 and you *still* don't know, figure it out – *like yesterday!*" Every day you lose at this end, you are also losing it at the other end of your life. Someone who is 40 now and lives to the ripe old age of 85 only has 45 summers left in their life! Why would you live your life *without* passion and exhilaration for what it is you are here to do on the planet?

Teach Life Skills

I am not minimizing the importance of traditional core subjects in our schooling systems, but there's a massive negative impact on our society from not teaching awareness-based training skills and fundamental life skills.

My vision for Co-Creative Schools and Co-Creative Universities embraces evolutionary teaching – providing education that evolves the consciousness of the human psyche. To me it is not a "nice to have" or about entertaining "progressive teachings." It is mission imperative to move with velocity to have those who have the power to make the difference, make the difference – *now*!

This Is A Leadership Imperative

Over the last twenty-two years, I've had the privilege of coaching many high-powered leaders. I use the three-legged stool analogy (see the model on page 168) to explain a key deficit:

The first leg of the stool is *traditional leadership*. These are the hard skills – the left-brain aspects of leadership. Most leaders are unconsciously competent in this area.

The second leg is *subject matter expertise*. Again, most leaders are unconsciously competent in the area within which they specialize.

The third leg is *mindset, behavioral change*. These are the soft skills – the right-brain aspects of leadership. These are often lumped into categories of "when we have the budget" or "when we have the time." Of course, this means they rarely get addressed. And yet, this is the most important leg of the stool where *sustainable change* is concerned.

Without strong foundations in any leg – and especially the third leg – the stool falls over. Leaders have a responsibility to grow and evolve in their leadership capability. Learn to be a leader who is always seeking to grow to be an evolved leader in the 21st century.

You will see in the model that ethics and values are at the base. If the foundations are unstable, ethics and values are in question.

Then you will see the four surrounding links connecting the base: Vision, Cultural Change, Commitment/Integrity, and Unrecognizable Transformation. They are connected because they are all essential to transformation:

Vision is integral to the direction and ethos of the culture.

Any cultural change process requires a high degree of commitment and integrity (sadly lacking in most organizations).

When commitment and integrity drive the change, the result is unrecognizable transformation.

Part of the ethos of the Co-Creative Age is to educate leaders on the importance of sustainable transformation. To not sustain change hinders the evolution of the human species.

LEADERSHIP THREE LEGGED STOOL ANALOGY

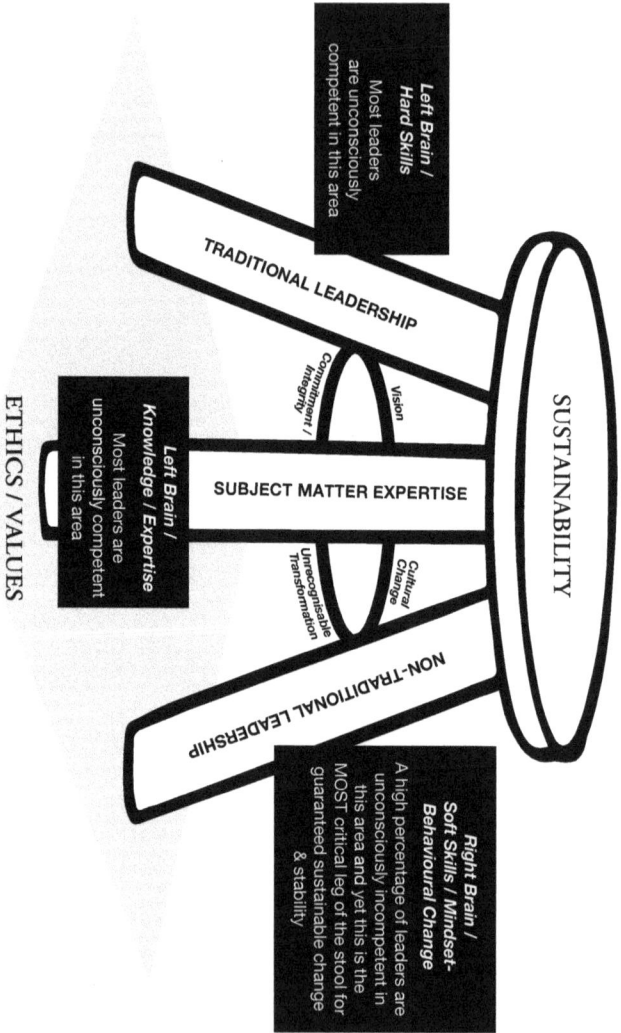

Left Brain / Hard Skills
Most leaders are unconsciously competent in this area

TRADITIONAL LEADERSHIP

Commitment / Integrity

Vision

ETHICS / VALUES

Left Brain / Knowledge / Expertise
Most leaders are unconsciously competent in this area

SUBJECT MATTER EXPERTISE

SUSTAINABILITY

Unrecognisable Transformation

Cultural Change

NON-TRADITIONAL LEADERSHIP

Right Brain / Soft Skills / Mindset- Behavioural Change
A high percentage of leaders are unconsciously incompetent in this area and yet this is the MOST critical leg of the stool for guaranteed sustainable change & stability

A Radical Change To The System

Sir Ken Robinson's 2006 TED Talk, *"Do schools kill creativity?"* is the most popular TED Talk of all time. When I last looked, it had 38 *million* views – and it continues to climb:

ted.com/talks/ken_robinson_says_schools_kill_creativity

It's astonishing that this simple presentation – without props, slides, or other visuals – has topped the TED charts, watched by more people than those delivered by political activists and pioneers of social change, mountaineers and deep-sea adventurers, scientists and visionaries.

Why such a hunger for a change in our schooling system? It's because deep down we *know* it's broken and inadequate.

In his four TED Talks to date, Ken Robinson addresses major problems in the system:

- *Do schools kill creativity?* A case for creating an education system that nurtures – rather than undermines – creativity.

- *Bring on the learning revolution!* Calling for a radical shift from standardized schools to personalized learning – so students' natural talents can flourish.

- *Changing education paradigms:* Three troubling trends in schools: rising drop-out rates, dwindling focus on the arts, and ADHD.

- *How to escape education's death valley:* Three principles crucial for the human mind to flourish – and how current education culture works against them.

Finland Leads The Way

These changes to the education system are not easy, but they are not impossible, either. In recent times, Finland's education system has caught worldwide attention – because Finnish students are leading international league tables of literacy and numeracy.

In Finland, schools are starting to focus more on life awareness skills rather than traditional academic subjects. Teaching traditional subjects – such as math and geography – is being phased out, and replaced by what the Finns call "phenomenon" teaching (teaching by topic). For example, students studying a hospitality course might attend a "cafeteria service" class, which includes math, writing, communication, and language skills.

The traditional classroom format – with rows of students sitting to attention and facing a teacher at the front – is also changing. Instead, students work together in smaller collaborative groups, learning important human-to-human interaction skills at the same time as their topics of study.

The changes in Finland are not only at the classroom level or school level, but through the entire education system – for example:

- Teachers are highly educated (they need at least a Master's degree) and respected.

- There are no mandatory texts and exams.

- Political leaders really do make education a high priority.

The Finnish model is not new, but is attracting interest from other leaders and educators around the world – although it will take a lot for them to actually make such radical changes.

Harvard University even offers a free online course, "Leading Change in Education Systems," which explores best practices from the most effective school systems around the world:

We are still a long way from all schools around the world adopting these ideas, but at least we're making progress because some leaders in education are considering that there is another way.

Recommendation

What relevance does this chapter have to you at this time? What difference can you specifically make? Why should you bother?

These are all relevant questions. Anyone who has ever made a difference on a global scale on this planet did not do it alone. It is only through the power of the collective that major change happens.

I will leave you with this question: If you – yes, you! – did have the power to make the difference, what would you do?

20

TRANSCENDENCE

There is a journey of a transformative nature to master oneself. Whether we take that journey or not is an individual choice in this lifetime.

I spoke in the first chapter, The Crazy Ones, of the movie 'Finding Joe', which beautifully depicts the story of the Hero's Journey – the stages of transformation developed by Joseph Campbell. If you have come this far in the book and not watched this movie, I highly recommend that you stop now and watch it, because it will make a significant difference in understanding this journey of self-mastery.

Let's Explore Further

All personal change is a journey of self-mastery.

When people come into any *change* process they want to *transition* from where they are operating to experience some level of *transformation*. At Co-creative Leadership, we believe you can go beyond that and experience a level of *transcendence*, where you completely change or alter in form. Some refer to this as transmutation or metamorphosis.

A high percentage of people operate at a lower, limited, level of consciousness, hanging out in their heads, making things mean things, operating from a default disempowered premise, in the known realm, living in what we term "past and future based projections." They wonder why life is showing up the way it is. Most do not realize how unconsciously they operate.

Let's dive deeper into understanding the journey of self-mastery and how it relates to you.

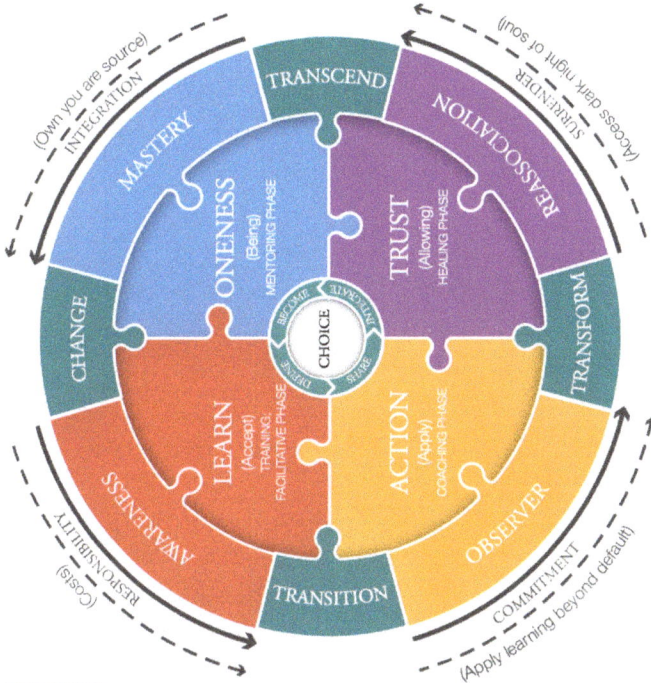

THE TRANSFORMATIONAL JOURNEY TO SELF-MASTERY

HIGHER LEVEL CONSCIOUSNESS — UNLIMITED POTENTIAL

POWER/POWER (Unknown World) Spiritual Being

LIVING IN THE NOW

FREE FALL

WORLD OF 'NO MEANING' CONNECTED - HEART SPACE

LOWER LEVEL CONSCIOUSNESS — LIMITED POTENTIAL

DEFAULT/DEFAULT (Known World) Human Being

LIVING IN THE PAST OR FUTURE

CLIFF FACE

WORLD OF 'MEANING' DISCONNECTED - HEAD SPACE

TRANSCEND · REASSOCIATION · TRANSFORM · OBSERVER · COMMITMENT (Apply learning beyond default) · TRANSITION · AWARENESS · RESPONSIBILITY (Costs) · CHANGE · INTEGRATION (Own you are source) · MASTERY · SURRENDER (Access dark night of soul)

ONENESS (Being) MENTORING PHASE · TRUST (Allowing) HEALING PHASE · ACTION (Apply) COACHING PHASE · LEARN (Accept) TRAINING FACILITATIVE PHASE

CHOICE · BECOME · INTEGRATE · BEING · DEFINE

The Journey To Self-Mastery

You will see a model for the journey to self-mastery on page 175. I'll explain it, starting from the top-left and continuing anti-clockwise.

Change To Transition

You will see there are three things that link each of the quadrants.

From CHANGE,
three things are critical for TRANSITION to take place:

1. You must be aware.

2. You must be willing to be responsible.

3. You must be present to the costs of where you are operating, fueling the need for change.

   If you're not transitioning from where you are now, it's because you're not aware, not wishing to take responsibility, and not being present to the costs of your destructive behavior.

   Being aware is not enough if you don't also choose to be responsible. To be responsible, you have to change your identity as you know it! Reframe responsibility as the ability to respond differently when you are aware.

   With all three elements in place, you can redefine who you are, and accept that there is another way. This is a training and facilitative stage, where you learn that change is finally possible.

Transition to Transformation

Most people I coach are in this phase. They are used to being coached, they are more evolved in their thinking (but still constrained), they are more of an observer in life than being reactive, they apply what they know within reason, and share who they are in the world. However, for whatever reason, they have found transformation (let alone sustainable transformation) elusive.

From TRANSITION to TRANSFORMATION, three things are critical:

1. You must be able to be the observer in every situation, without being affected by external circumstances. That's being equanimous!

2. You must move beyond just *wanting* transformation to being *committed* to it. Most people want to play on the court called "Want," but want the results from the court called "Committed." In case you haven't noticed, *this is not possible!* Most people have no concept of what it takes to be committed. *Ouch!*

3. You must apply what you know *beyond* your default. If you don't know you have a default identity, it sabotages your potential – and that's why transformation is elusive. Most people who come into the Co-creative Leadership education are highly trained, and have "been there and done that" personally and professionally. However, for whatever reason, most have not experienced the transformation they want nor know how to sustain it.

Co-creative Leadership is the only global leadership development service provider that not only specializes in sustainable transformation both personally and professionally, but also teaches how to transform your default disempowered identity permanently.

After you truly master what it means to observe, learn the nuances of what it takes to be committed, and learn at an integral level the makeup of your individual default identity, you can experience the transformation you so richly deserve.

Quadrants 1 and 2 are what we call "1-to-3 dimensional thinking": still living in the realm of man-made meaning.

Transformation to Transcendence

This is where you raise your consciousness to new levels and to limitless potential. You reconnect at a heart level in the realm of no default-based meaning, and experience living a sustained empowered existence, as a spiritual being, trusting the unknown implicitly, living in the now moment.

This is the most difficult phase to describe, because you are trying to understand something that fundamentally can only be *experienced.*

Many people ask:

- How do I trust?

- How do I let go?

- How do I surrender?

None of the answers to these questions lies in the known realm – the thinking realm, the realm of knowledge.

For example, the person who goes bungy jumping has a completely different experience from the person who watches them do it. The observer cannot fathom the experience unless they have experienced what it felt like to let go, trust, and surrender.

Going beyond transformation to experience transcendence requires you to do three things:

- Re-associate back into being whole and complete.

- Surrender and let go of the known realm to experience the magic in the unknown realm.

- Access the dark night of the soul (sounds dramatic, doesn't it?), which means getting out of your head and getting into your heart.

This is another way of living – one where you are integrated and allowing new possibilities to appear in your life.

The idea of healing (and I'm not referring to counseling or psychotherapy) has mixed reviews and mixed acceptance. In traditional leadership teachings, there is no focus on "healing" being integral to leadership development. A leader is a human being. A leader who is not integrated and not healed cannot achieve their ultimate potential. *Fact!*

Co-creative Leadership is the only global leadership development provider that advocates healing and coaching together to experience full reintegration. Coaching in isolation is not sustainable. Healing in isolation is not sustainable. The two together: formidable!

There needs to be more education in the marketplace to educate leaders on the benefits of healing, including these:

- It provides an understanding of self at an integral level as to what is holding you back.

- It heals anything from your past.

- It enables you to experience a reconnection to self that can only be learned through experience.

- Finally, it enables you to sustain the change you have always wanted in your life without your past sabotaging your future.

Regardless of how great your childhood was, you can benefit from healing to help you with full reintegration to self.

Transcendence

The final stage, TRANSCENDENCE, is the ultimate – the elixir or the arrival. It's what some refer to as self-actualization.

You have reached a level of *mastery*, and you become unrecognizable to yourself. You own that you are part of the whole, and there is no separateness in the *oneness* of being. You *become* your vision. You have fully integrated back into being whole and complete.

This is what The Co-Creative Age accomplishes. It's a world where we as a race experience this level of consciousness as the *norm* – not just accessible by a token few.

For this to be experienced more widely as a culture, we need to teach the way to experience this level of existence – hence the establishment of Co-Creative Schools and Co-Creative Universities.

Quadrants 3 and 4 are what we call "4th/5th dimensional thinking and beyond," where you are continuously evolving to unfathomable levels.

We Can Evolve Beyond The Need For Adversity

In our current level of consciousness, we use adversity as our primary way of learning and evolving as a human species.

In my first book, *'Freefall – Living Life Beyond The Edge'*, I introduce the term "culturalization," a world where we no longer need to manifest adversity to learn. I had to experience thirty years of extreme adversity to learn what I have learned to now teach that "There Is Another Way!"

People ask me, "Surely adversity is the only way we learn – isn't it a good thing?" At this level of consciousness, I agree. But I'm talking about something different. If we were to elevate the mass consciousness, there would be no need to operate and manifest adversity as our only vehicle to evolve.

If I gave you a Rubik's Cube and asked you to solve it, you probably couldn't – except by ripping off all the stickers and putting them back in a different order. Erno Rubik's ingenious invention has 43 quintillion variations (if I showed you one every second, it would take 100 times the life of the universe to show them all) and its solution is rooted in an advanced branch of mathematics called group theory.

Yet you could watch a ten-minute YouTube video that teaches you a step-by-step process for solving it, and then you can easily solve it yourself – every time – in under three minutes.

My unique life apprenticeship has taught me the proven step-by-step process. I had to go through what I did to be able to teach this now, but I know now that adversity isn't the sole vehicle. There *is* another way.

Recommendation

We are born with free will and choice. We will either listen to the call to live to our fullest potential in this lifetime or deny it. It's a bit like *The Matrix*, where you have the decision to take the red pill or the blue pill. Which will you take?

21

PAY IT
FORWARD

f you have worked your way up to a senior leadership position, you probably had the benefits of working with some wise mentors along the way. There's a lot of talk about mentoring in leadership training now, and that's not surprising, because having a mentor has a lot of advantages:

- They share their real-life experience with you.

- They see potential in you that you can't see in yourself.

- They help you make better decisions when facing different paths.

- They introduce you to influential people in their networks.

- They act as a sounding board when you're confused and seeking clarity.

- They offer impartial advice and guidance.

Those are all powerful benefits for you as the student or mentoree, but what about the benefits for the mentor? Why did they invest their valuable time and expertise – probably unpaid – to help you?

If you have worked your way up to a senior leadership position, you probably mentored other people along their path as well. Why did *you* do it?

Of course, mentors learn and grow as part of the mentoring experience, and some say they learn as much as – if not more than – the people they mentor. But the biggest benefit of being a mentor is the ability to pay it forward – to share your experience, knowledge, and wisdom with somebody else.

This Is Our Ultimate Purpose

The main purpose in our human existence is to not only follow our calling and fulfill on it, but to then pay forward what we have learned. When you evolve to a higher level of consciousness and awareness, your journey isn't complete. There's still the opportunity and obligation to pay it forward.

Think about the opportunity missed due to the lack of awareness-based education in the marketplace. Leaders who don't evolve and then don't pay forward their knowledge are ripping off the planet.

As I said earlier, I often say to people who experience our education, "I am not solely interested in *your* transformation! I am more interested in the lives you are here to transform when you get out of the way!"

To deny what you are being called to do on this planet is not serving those that you were put here on planet Earth to serve.

Remember Your Calling

Marianne Williamson was famously quoted as writing:

"Our deepest fear is not that we are inadequate. Our deepest fear is that we are powerful beyond measure. It is our light, not our darkness that most frightens us. We ask ourselves, 'Who am I to be brilliant, gorgeous, talented, fabulous?' Actually, who are you not to be?"

Some people deny the calling, and default into "I'm *not* brilliant, gorgeous, talented, or fabulous." They create that reality, not even realizing they are doing so.

Some have followed the calling, but come up against tests that confront them with their humanness. If they don't have the skills to know how to transition, they go back into the realm of unconsciousness.

And then there's the third group of people, who have followed the call, tipped to the higher level of consciousness, stayed the distance, and seen their vision come to fruition.

Again, this isn't mystic mumbo-jumbo. You have seen examples in people (see Chapter 2), businesses, organizations, and even states and nations.

For example, there are organizations that invent something transformative, enter the market late but dominate it, operate from a radically different corporate culture, rise up from the ashes, or grow from a two-bit operation to a global powerhouse.

Almost without exception, these people and organizations who achieve success then pay it forward – for example:

- Google, a late entrant to the search engine market but now a dominant player, invests in projects to connect humanity and transform the planet.

- Billionaire Silicon Valley technology investor Vinod Khosla uses his wealth to invest in startup companies that are transforming healthcare.

- Manoj Bhargava, the founder of 5 Hour Energy. In 2015, he pledged to give 99 percent of his wealth to philanthropic causes. His foundations include the Hans Foundation and Rural India Supporting Trust. In 2016, Bhargava told National Geographic that he planned to distribute 10,000 of his stationary, power-generating bikes to rural homes and villages in India.

Get Out Of Your Story

Everybody has a story, and nobody has the right to judge anybody else's story. What they are going through is relative to and relevant for that individual.

But I often say to people, "You are never given anything you can't handle." In fact, it's my byline and the subtitle of my keynote presentation to business leaders.

I'm a living, breathing example of somebody who was given something that most people would not recover from or survive, but I did. I know that whatever hand you have been dealt, you're never given anything you can't handle.

Your living, breathing example of that is yourself. The fact you're alive and reading this now proves it. You might have experienced many trials and tests in your personal or professional life – such as bankruptcy, dishonesty from inside and outside the organization, being overlooked for promotion, divorce, death of loved ones, life-threatening illness, and so on. And yet you're here now. Whatever it was, you handled it.

When you look back on those events, you might notice you handled them by getting out of the story. When it happened, you were living it – it *was* your story. But to handle it and transcend it, you had to get out of the story.

"You are *not* your story but it does form the backbone of your character on how you show up in the world."

Sally Anderson

This Is Your Life Apprenticeship

Every human being has a story, and your story is your life apprenticeship. Whether or not you learn through that apprenticeship is up to you. As a leader, part of your leadership contract is to use your story, learn from it, and pay forward the learnings.

What you're here to learn is what you're here to teach.

I had to learn at an extreme, severe level to trust, let go, and surrender. At first, I didn't trust, I didn't let go, and I certainly didn't surrender. Yet that's what I teach now.

When you achieve that level of leadership, you not only pay it forward, you also become stable in who you are and an inspiration to those you lead.

Add It To Your Organization's Strategy

Many organizations have lofty statements proclaiming their mission, vision, and values. But more often than not, these lofty statements don't mean anything to the people in the organization.

But when you add an element of paying it forward to your mission, *now* you have something worth aspiring to.

This is the point of Simon Sineks popular Ted Talk entitled, Start with Why, which has more than twenty-five million views – **https://www.youtube.com/watch?v=2Ss78LfY3nE**

Your "Why" underpins everything else, and when it involves paying it forward, it's inspiring. When your entire purpose for being 24/7 is to answer the question "What difference have you made in another's life today?", that's a very inspiring approach to business.

For example, here are some truly inspiring pay-it-forward mission statements – all from for-profit businesses:

- **Ann Taylor:** "To inspire and connect with women to put their best selves forward every day."

- **Aveda:** "To care for the world we live in, from the products we make to the ways in which we give back to society."

- **Facebook:** "To make the world more open and connected."

- **Google:** "To organize the world's information and make it universally accessible and useful."

- **Life is Good:** "To spread the power of optimism."

- **Patagonia:** "To use business to inspire, and implement solutions to the environmental crisis."

- **Seventh Generation:** "To inspire a consumer revolution that nurtures the health of the next seven generations."

- **TOMS Shoes:** "To help improve lives."

- **Twitter:** "To give everyone the power to create and share ideas and information instantly, without barriers."

It is the most priceless vocation on the planet when you wake every day knowing you're changing lives and helping future generations.

Even if you can only change one person at a time – starting with yourself – that ripple effect will affect everybody, including future generations that aren't even here yet.

The Power of Philanthropy

At Co-creative Leadership we are driven by the power of philanthropy.

The three causes that I am standing for are:

1. For over twenty years, I dedicated my life philanthropically to eradicating teen suicide; our kids are dying and it's not okay. The fact that we tolerate the level of disassociation in our global society to the teen suicide statistics is a crime.

2. I am also very clear I have a systemic part to play at ending the heinous crimes against our youngest children that lies in the silence in our society, i.e., paedophilia, child trafficking, baby bashing, baby killings. There will be a time where we will no longer permit these abominable crimes to exist.

3. Advocating for ending all cruelty to animals . . .

You Never Know ...

Over twenty-two years, I made a decision that at the time I did not realize would have a great impact on my life: I decided that if I saw something I could compliment a person about, instead of just thinking it, I would say it.

I remember once when I was sitting in a restaurant with some coach trainees, and an elderly woman walked in. She was that beautiful – really distinguished – and I couldn't help but be taken by her beauty. So, true to form, I went over to her table and acknowledged her for her beauty.

About 10 minutes later, a waiter came over and delivered a glass of champagne. I asked who it was from, then looked up and saw the distinguished lady waving at me.

About an hour later, she and her husband came to the table; she looked me straight in the eye and said, "You have no idea what a difference you made in my life today!" When I asked how, she replied, "My son died today."

This reminded me yet again that you never know what's happening in someone else's world. My point is it doesn't take much to pay forward your wisdom, your compliments, your love, and your energy *daily*. If you stopped focusing only on yourself and the dynamics playing out in the company, and focused more on how you can serve, this would be a transformed planet.

Recommendation

What about you and your organization? To what degree do you
have a conscience about the part you play in paying it forward?
Instead of a scarcity mindset based on ruthless competition,
believe in a co-opetive mindset that genuinely wants to pay it
forward. If you are already taking action, I commend you! If you are
not, I highly recommend tabling this as a priority strategy within
your business.

Also, there is a *big* difference between "looking good
philanthropy" and genuine philanthropy. Which do you choose?

Watch the "Pay It Forward" movie:

https://www.youtube.com/watch?v=URwXr144hll

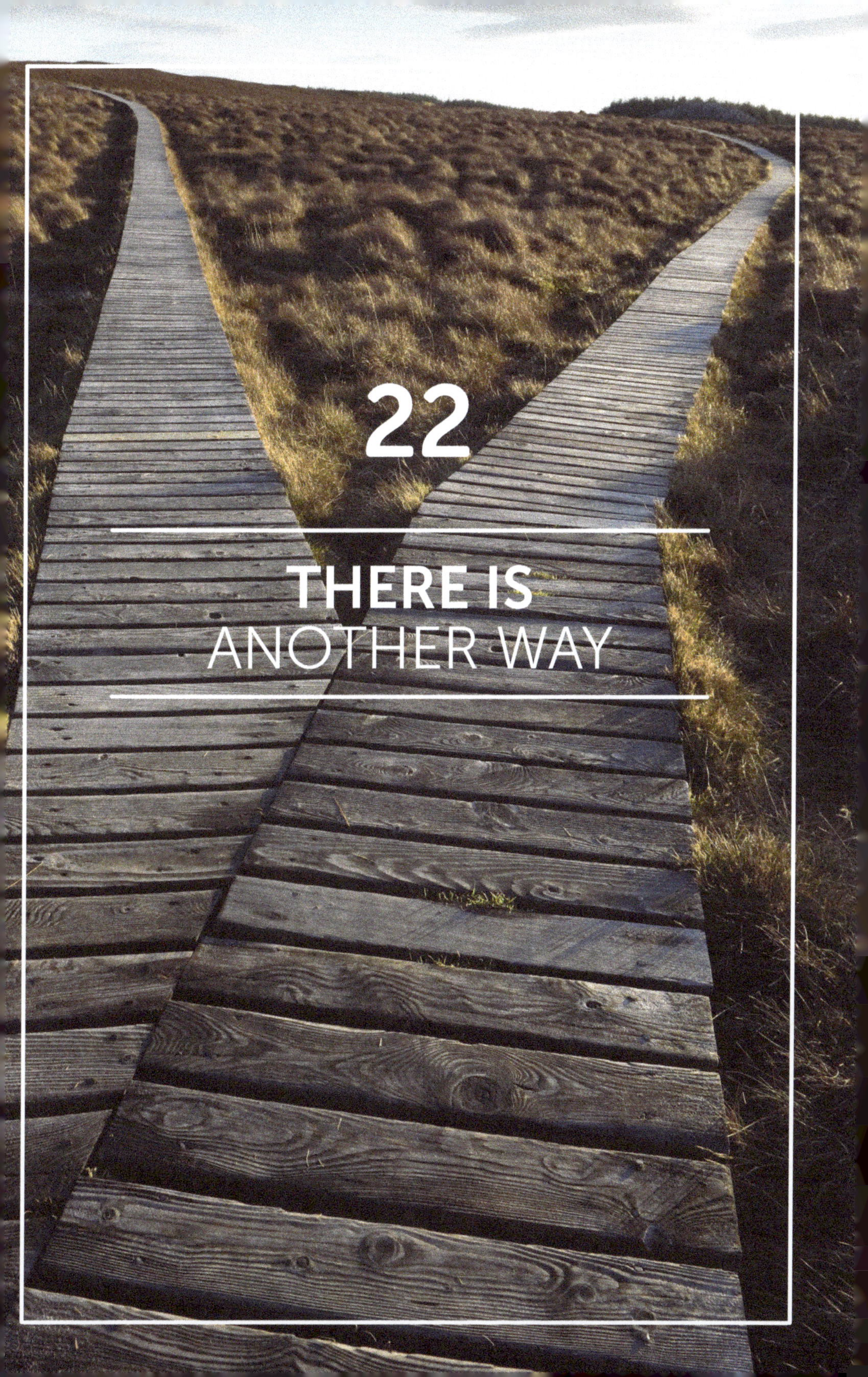

22

THERE IS ANOTHER WAY

Consider the cost of keeping one human being in the prison system, the cost of maintaining one human being who has never been able to get paid employment, or the cost of one unwanted teenage pregnancy.

As a society, we pay a huge price for dysfunction. Where is the logic that you can get paid more to be unemployed than for being employed? Where is the logic in keeping someone medicated and dependent on the system, rather than providing viable healing solutions so they can be an active, productive member of society? Where is the logic in prescribing anti-depression drugs to infants or five- to eight- year-olds (Are you kidding me???)

I believe we have a solution – a sustainable solution – to the dysfunction in our society.

There is another way.

It's now time to have this education in the hands of those who are able to change the human condition at a causal level – not just a symptomatic level.

I'm not saying I'm the fount of all knowledge, and I'm not criticizing the sincere efforts of what has gone before. But I *am* saying we have another solution, and one that goes deep into the evolution of the human psyche.

I'm also saying we *need* another way. As the saying goes,

"Insanity is doing the same thing over and over again, and expecting different results."

Start With The School System

As I discussed in Chapter 19, this must start with the education system.

Specifically, I want every single child coming through the education system to understand their default identity.

I talked earlier about Abraham Maslow and his famous "Hierarchy of Needs" – with self-actualization at the highest level:

- Biological and physiological needs – such as air, food, shelter, sleep, and sex

- Safety needs – such as security, law, order, stability, and freedom from fear

- Love and belongingness needs – such as friendship, intimacy, affection, and love

- Esteem needs – such as achievement, mastery, independence, self-respect, and respect from others

- Self-actualization needs – such as realizing personal potential, self-fulfillment, seeking personal growth, and peak experiences

I firmly believe it's a tragedy that so few people walking the planet are self-actualized.

The point of Maslow's hierarchy is that it *is* a hierarchy: You can't progress to higher levels until you have your lower-level needs satisfied. As long as people continue operating from their default, dependent on the social welfare system or dependent on drugs that we endorse as a society, they will languish at the lower levels.

Let's Pour Money Into *This* Research

I realize it's not easy to flick a switch and expect every education system on the planet to change *for no reason at all*. But change does happen instantly when there's motivation to change.

For centuries, Europeans believed all swans were white – until they came to Australia and saw black swans. Instantly, the definition of a swan changed to accommodate the new evidence.

I would love it if everybody trusted the unknown and acted without evidence, but most people on the planet do need evidence before they act.

So let's get the evidence.

When universities or private research groups see the potential in something that could be a game changer – a new technology, a cure for cancer, or the discovery of another Earth-like planet – they invest in it. So let's invest in the research in this area as well.

Right now, there is so much resistance to the idea of accepting – let alone trusting – the unknown realm. If we need to find the evidence, let's find it. Let's show them the path.

It's All A Matter Of Time

I know I am alive today to give back what I have learned. I also know my legacy in this lifetime is for this education to live beyond me. So I have taken liberties in this book to be frank, to be "open kimono" in my communication style, to say what I know is right.

It is just a matter of time before the education I have spent a lifetime developing is in the hands of those committed to enhancing the human condition on a mass level.

Does it take something to overcome your naysayers, your own conditioning and belief systems, the well-meaning friend, or the caring family member? Hell, *yes!* But when you are called, you have no choice but to transcend your own limited thinking (and theirs).

Brené Brown, a research professor at the University of Houston Graduate College of Social Work, says:

"If you're not in the arena getting your butt kicked too, I'm not interested in your feedback."

If you are prepared to get into the arena and know what it feels like, then – and only then – will I consider what you have to say is of value.

I am in the arena, and have been for many years. My vocation is coaching leaders not only on how to get into the arena and show up, but to accomplish their game plan in the arena. There is nowhere else to be in this lifetime but in the arena.

If you are reading this book, you know that it is your responsibility to not only get into the arena but to stay in the arena, because the game can only be won in the arena!

"It is not the critic who counts: not the man who points out how the strong man stumbles or where the doer of deeds could have done better. The credit belongs to the man who is actually **in the arena**, whose face is marred by dust and sweat and blood, who strives valiantly, who errs and comes up short again and again, because there is no effort without error or shortcoming, but who knows the great enthusiasms, the great devotions, who spends himself in a worthy cause; who, at the best, knows, in the end, the triumph of high achievement, and who, at the worst, if he fails, at least he fails while daring greatly, so that his place shall never be with those cold and timid souls who knew neither victory nor defeat."

—Theodore Roosevelt

Recommendation

Watch Brené Brown's presentation, "Why Your Critics Aren't The Ones Who Count":

https://www.youtube.com/watch?v=8-JXOnFOXQk

23

THE CO-CREATIVE
SUMMIT

Most of this book has been about urging you – a leader with significant influence, authority, and control over organizations and your people – to follow your calling and consider that there is another way.

We are not alone. We do have transformative leaders on the planet now. We do have the ability to make a difference now.

People with shared interests and goals do come together all the time – for meetings, conferences, retreats, and summits. Even with the growth of video conferencing, virtual reality, and holograms, the meetings industry is alive and thriving, because we still want to meet in person. We still *need* to meet.

Most leaders meet around a table in a boardroom. Some transformative leaders share their ideas from a stage with audiences hungry for change. Only a few collaborate to create change. It fascinates me that we have the awareness and consciousness on the planet now, yet most people in the transformative field don't collaborate to the degree they could.

I have an idea.

Part of my 20-year vision is to host one of the most powerful co-creative summits the world has ever seen.

I call on 50 of the top transformative leaders on this planet to congregate in Queenstown, in the South Island of New Zealand. Queenstown is a spiritual place, like Sedona in the USA, and is the ideal place to host this summit.

I attended a Wisdom Summit many years ago in New Zealand where Neale Donald Walsch, the author of the series, *'Conversations with God'*, presented. He stated that New Zealand would be the future destination of spiritual leadership on this planet, and it resonated then as it does now.

The guest list would include the likes of Anthony Robbins, Dr. John Demartini, Eckhart Tolle, Robin Sharma, Deepak Chopra, Marianne Williamson, Oprah Winfrey ... the list goes on.

This is not a talk-fest; in fact, it's just the opposite. I believe that much of the summit needs to be held in silence. Can you imagine the collective power of that group channeling what needs to be channeled?

It's amazing that in most Western cultures, business meetings are full of talk and very little silence. Yet in Japanese business meetings, after somebody talks, it's common for the rest of the group to sit in silence – absorbing, reflecting, and engaging with the thought just expressed. That's the dynamic that leads to powerful shifts.

I believe we have the collective power to channel what is needed as we evolve as a human collective, but for this to occur we need to listen . . .

Do Whatever It Takes

My ultimate wish is for this Summit to become a reality. This book is an important step on that journey. What "call to action" would be required to elicit interest from those who can make the difference on this planet *now*? And now I ask you, the reader!

Legacy is the most profound conversation you can facilitate with a human being on the planet. What are *you* doing here? What is your DNA calling you to be in the world?

I believe that whatever you receive, regardless of how bizarre it seems, is meant to be heard. As a leader, trust implicitly what you receive intuitively.

The idea of the Co-Creative Summit and my 20 Year Vision came to me in about 10–15 minutes in 2010. I believe without question that it's part of my destiny to honor what was received.

Recommendation

We have a solution to wake people up, have them fulfill the legacy of why they are here, and pay it forward. That has the ability to transform the planet!

Watch Martin Luther King Jr.'s I Have a Dream speech, one of the most iconic visionaries of our time.

https://www.youtube.com/watch?v=vP4iY1TtS3s

24

EVOLVED LEADERSHIP

The leadership landscape post-pandemic globally has changed. We will not be returning to what was. Of the many negatives with Covid-19, some of the positives are openness, awareness, association to embracing new approaches, new innovation, new ways of doing things, especially the way in which we lead.

Soft skills, or what I prefer to call 'human skills' prior to Covid-19 were entertained but not taken seriously. Concepts like compassion, empathy, kindness are not new concepts, people, but they are now ironically embraced in a way like never before that enhances not only the human condition but performance, productivity, and effectiveness.

Sad that it took a pandemic to awaken the acceptance and importance of looking at ALL FACETS of what it means to be the 'whole human.' Less of the head-based, linear, hard skills of traditional leadership and more towards the heart-based, nonlinear, soft skills way of leadership.

The timing of the co-creative approach is now. To lead from the humanistic form is limited, to lead from the co-creative form is limitless in potential. I have said it before and I will say it again, to solve the new world problems on our doorstep, let alone those that are coming that haven't even eventuated yet, we need to urgently fast-track the evolution of consciousness of those who lead.

Albert Einstein was right; no problem can be solved from the same level of consciousness that created it!

I believe there needs to be more openness to:

- <u>Healing</u> for leaders, for we have a lot of little boys and little girls running businesses, economies, and countries who have not done the deep work.

- Talking about the importance of <u>faith</u> (whatever that is for you) as an integral business practice.

- Providing <u>sustainable solutions</u> to the growing epidemic of mental health issues globally—there will come a time when the suicide statistics will no longer be a number and we will associate to the critical importance of offering viable long-term solutions and alternatives to those struggling with their mental state.

- Teaching leaders how to <u>embrace uncertainty</u> so that they can navigate with confidence versus fear.

- The importance of <u>love</u> in business at all levels, considering every ecosystem, be that corporate, government, or business, is a makeup of human beings and there is not one person on the planet who doesn't want to feel love, know love, experience love. Compartmentalising love as something that is only personal and not appropriate in business is ludicrous.

- Fundamentally changing what we <u>teach in schools</u> globally to change the way we as humans function and evolve.

- <u>Not tolerating war</u> as the solution to solving conflict between countries—we as humans are supposed to be the most evolved creatures/race on the planet and yet we still keep killing each other ?????

- <u>Ending the bureaucracy of governments</u> not being held to account to solve the biggest issues facing this planet.

- <u>Stopping the pharmaceutical stronghold</u>—looking at new ways to address the causal dynamics creating the symptoms instead of numbing them.

- <u>Infiltrating the silence</u> that endorses the acceptance of heinous crimes to our children, i.e., paedophilia, child trafficking, baby bashing, baby killing, etc.

- <u>Ending all cruelty to animals</u>—animals have a lot to teach us humans who inflict such pain.

- <u>Taking climate change seriously</u> instead of expecting the planet to sustain the degree of harm we inflict on it every single day.

I could keep going but you get the gist . . .

As the landscape changes, so too, do we. Trying to return to 'business as usual,' post-pandemic is the height of ignorance. There is a level of complacency in existence currently that thinks we have time, but alas this is not the case. There is a sense of urgency needed.

The Co-creative Age—The Next Evolutionary Phase in Leadership advocates for systemic change, for our survival as a global society depends on it.

There comes a time when expending more dollars on resources, forums, and reports to think about, talk about the issues will not cut it. The fact that we tolerate this as a society speaks volumes for the level of disassociation at play.

We have a responsibility to be courageous enough to stand for new possibilities in the face of mass resistance to change at this level. I, for one, will spend the rest of my life being an advocate for enhancing the human condition to do better.

Recommendation

As John Lennon sang in *Imagine*:

"You may say I'm a dreamer
But I'm not the only one
I hope some day you'll join us,
And the world will be as one."

"Courage is having a love affair
with the unknown."

Osho

About Sally Anderson

Sally Anderson: Trusted Advisor | Confidante | Speaker | Author | Leading Authority @ The Forefront of Sustainable 'Human & Organisational' Transformation

Founder of Equanimity & Co-Creative Mastery and Visionary Force of Nature to The Elite

Many coaches and advisors claim to guide clients to transcend limitations and achieve unprecedented growth, but none have survived the unfathomable, done the unexpected, and dared to go to the places Sally Anderson is willing to go as the only documented visionary at the forefront of sustainable human and organizational transformation.

Sally's understanding of the human psyche and her ability to use these insights to enhance the way in which leaders lead places her as one of the greatest leadership influencers of our time. With a legacy built on over thirty years of professional leadership experience, working with thousands of CEOs, politicians, leading-edge thought leaders, elite sporting athletes, and global influencers, Sally is known as the professional sparring partner to influential leaders who expect quantifiable results from the very first engagement.

Sally's program, Equanimity & Co-Creative Mastery is an experiential, meticulously planned, heavily tested methodology developed for elite performers, global brands, and world changers to achieve sustainable and previously unattainable results. Her work in the area of 'sustainable transformation' is unparalleled.

Sally's journey has been riddled with challenges no human

should be forced to endure-surviving unthinkable traumas, overcoming mental dysfunction, and even weathering an attempted character assassination. Her resilience, though, is a testament to her authenticity, spirit, and commitment to her purpose. Her ability to transform adversity into growth, to rebuild a global network, and provide much needed guidance to the most influential and misunderstood means Sally's story is one that continues to inspire and lead.

Based in New Zealand, and operating 100 percent worldwide, Sally selectively takes on private and consulting clients while curating intimate, life-altering events during her travels. Her availability extends to speaking engagements, facilitation at aligned high-end leadership retreats/masterclasses, and collaborations where there is an acute need to unleash unstoppable potential and conquer limitations in those with influence.

Discover more at sallyandersoninternational.com—authorized access available on application.

Inquire about Sally's coaching, speaking, consultancy services via her management: kathryn.porritt@iconicinfluencers.com.

SALLY ANDERSON

Sally Anderson International
Based in New Zealand/USA
2450 Lakeside Pkwy, Flower Mound,
Texas, 75022, United States of America

LinkedIn: https://www.linkedin.com/in/sallyanderson-worldclass-coach-intuitive/

Email: sally@sallyandersoninternational.com

Website: www.sallyandersoninternational.com

Who Sally Coaches

Three decades in the leadership trenches, twenty-two years of which in private practice (at time of writing this) as a leadership coach to the influencers

HIGHLY TRAINED INDIVIDUALS

Those striving to become (HNWI – High Net worth Individuals) who have tried everything in the marketplace personally and/or professionally but struggle to not only attain the desired level of transformation they seek but understand how to sustain said change-the more responsible and aware humanity is the more they will pay forward their knowledge to their fellowman.

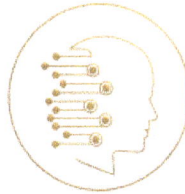

HIGH END CEOS / C-SUITE EXECUTIVES

Post-Covid, traditional leadership, as we know it, is dead. We will not be returning to the linear, hard skills realm of leadership. Most leaders are used to being in control; many do not know how to navigate the domain of uncertainty. Now more than ever, there is a need to evolve the consciousness of those who lead at the highest level to solve the new world problems.

Albert Einstein quoted: **"We can't solve problems by using the same kind of thinking we used when we created them." – entrée Co-creative/Equanimous Leadership.**

No one can sustain the superhuman expectations placed on them from EVERY quarter. Yet, day in and day out, the expectation remains. Ever notice how mental health is palatable to talk about in the workplace at an employee level but NOT in the context of senior executive leadership? Stigmatisation exists, which I'm on a mission to eliminate.

POLITICIANS

The new era of politics requires politicians to STOP bagging the opposition and to spend more quality time educating their constituents on their specific policies and to implement as a priority proactive 'succession planning,' so we have viable candidates to vote for–this currently is a global issue.

ELITE SPORTING ATHLETES

With the increase in social media trolling and cancel culture the need to know how to navigate the terrain of the media takes something. Not to mention how to recalibrate when the ball doesn't go your way in front of millions of raving fans real-time. To provide a different level of cadence and performance that is sustainable is a higher leveraged value proposition unique to the equanimous/co-creative mastery approach.

GLOBAL INFLUENCERS | THOUGHT LEADERS | CHANGE AGENTS | PIONEERS | RABBLE-ROUSERS | LUMINARIES | BIG THINKERS | INSTIGATORS | PEACEMAKERS | INVENTORS

Sally coaches the brightest minds in the world to share 'their unique wisdom' for igniting a healthier, more prosperous society, and a better life on this planet, for it will be these leaders who will create the new future!

CELEBRITIES

Instead of going in and out of rehabilitation centres, learn the art of sustaining change unique to Sally's education and elevate your purpose for making the planet a better place.

MILITARY FORCES

Sally's passion project is providing a non-drug related solution to replace the issues surrounding PTSD drug dependency.

MILLIONAIRES / BILLIONAIRES

Due to the high level of dissatisfaction facing a high percentage of millionaires and billionaires, even in the face of supposedly having everything, there is a need for this sector of the market to take more responsibility, to give back, and honour their contribution to societal

issues facing the planet.

Services

- Six-twelve month private one-to-one Co-creative Leadership Partnership Coaching Programs

- Twelve-Month Equanimous Leadership Immersion Programs

- Three-Day Co-creative Leadership Retreats

- One-Day High End Leadership Masterclasses

- Leadership Development Consultancy

What People Say

"I've been a speaker for over 20 years in the USA and I have never seen a more compelling speaker than Sally Anderson."

Alex Carroll, Radio Publicity Guru, USA, radiopublicity.com

"In a world where so many speakers are self-proclaimed experts, Sally stands out as one of those rare speakers who have actually earned the right to grace the stage. A master of personal growth and sustainable transformation, Sally combines her high-impact and electrifying presence with an intimate and personal connection to her audience to create an experience that stirs the imagination of every soul in the room. When I watched Sally on the stage in Los Angeles, I was riveted by her ability to take her horrific story, frame it perfectly for the audience so that they could receive it, and then share her triumph to a screaming standing ovation. Every person in that room carried a piece of Sally with them when they left. I have spoken to some who were in that audience and her impact on their lives remains long after she leaves the stage."

Steve Lowell, Past President of Global Speakers Association

Sally is a lightning bolt with a direct connection to the primal source. Her abilities and gifts are literally transcendent on every level. She's a Gandalf, a powerful white wizard on this planet. That's as close as I can get to a description that comes anywhere close to doing justice with words. For those who seek the privilege/opportunity of working with Sally, rest assured, she doesn't play games and doesn't waste time. She goes straight to the heart of any matter and gets results that many coaches or therapists can't achieve in two lifetimes. Like a mother lioness,

Sally understands the brutality of the world, the high stakes at hand, and prepares you for the true fight with simultaneous tenderness and ferocity. If you have developed yourself to a certain point of readiness, she is the IDEAL addition to your arsenal-one who understands how every moment on this planet counts and asks you, "What do you need to do next?"

If you need to find your big WHY, if you have held yourself back because of pain, or if you need to supercharge your next leap into profound uplevel, expect the magic to reveal itself when you connect with Sally.

Jennifer Burnham Grubbs – Founder of Quantum Insurance, Los Angeles, USA

Sally Anderson is truly a visionary at the forefront of sustainable human and organizational transformation. I have never met such an intuitive and powerful coach who ignites leaders to become more impassioned, and to evolve leaders to a new level of awareness for the purposes of liberating themselves to new levels of performance. Sally is also the most generous and gracious of leaders, paying it forward to champion others, and cocreating innovative breakthroughs.

For those looking for sustainable, leading-edge performance, Sally has an astonishing track record of creating effective organizational and personal transformations, which is why she is the trusted advisor to key influencers, nationally and internationally, for over twenty years, including CEOs, politicians, global influencers, visionaries, celebrities, and billionaires. Every world-class leader shaping industry, policy, and innovation needs Sally as their secret weapon!

Sally's unique personal perspectives, along with her traumatic history, have supported her eventual mastery as a transformational coach. Her rare combination of talents led her to become one of the most pre-eminent speakers and transformation coaches globally. Sally is an incredible gift to her clients, as well as everyone who is lucky enough to connect with her. I highly recommend Sally Anderson, without reservation.

Linda Fisk/Chairwoman – LeadHERship Global, Texas, USA

Sally Anderson is a powerhouse to be reckoned with. Her direct approach with relentless commitment to cocreating innovative breakthrough makes her a sought after coach and consultant to executives, politicians, and influencers. Collaborating with her is a unique journey that brings out the best in all involved.

Drawing from her lived experiences, Sally demonstrates a knack for shaping effective organizational and personal transformations. I have watched her work her magic on clients and experienced her tenacious initiative commitment to excellence. Every world class leader needs Sally as their secret weapon!

My serendipitous connection with Sally evolved into a professional relationship and organically blossomed into a deeply meaningful friendship. I know I can lean in for authentic guidance from her and so can you. I highly recommend Sally Anderson, without reservation.

Kasthuri Henry, PHD, CTP, Six Sigma Black Belt/Founder of Ennobling for Success/Social Entrepreneur/University Lecturer – Belize, Caribbean

Sally Anderson is truly one of the most remarkable leaders, trailblazers, and humans I have met on this entire planet. The combination of her profound wisdom, knowledge, diverse experience, transformative gifts to advising and mentoring with top leaders, politicians, and influencers makes her an exceptional gem and truly one of a kind as she is someone who I have had the honour and pleasure of knowing personally and professionally. Sally's contributions, commitment, dedication, deliverables, and heart to serve humanity and make long-lasting change are unparalleled as she is one of the most dynamic visionaries, behavioural experts, human performance specialists, and top executive legacy coaches I have ever met in my many years of international leadership coaching and advising. I highly recommend Sally; in particular, if you are a high-level leader looking to take your life and business to newfound levels you never dreamed were possible!

Nadene Joy - Executive Leadership Coach and Advisor, Strategic Partnerships, Economic Assessment Geologist - Saskatchewan, Canada

Having interviewed well over one thousand Thoughts Leaders over the last decade across multiple countries, disciplines, and industries, Sally Anderson is truly a standout, which is why I had no hesitation to get her back on my podcast for a sequel within a few weeks of the first episode.

Sally is a true thought leader and is undoubtably at the forefront of her industry, specialising in cultural transformation at individual and organisational levels.

Her body of work is a global first as it focuses on the 'sustainability' element of personal and professional transformation.

Something, I've not seen nor had any of my other guests speak about, as this has been developed over her two-decades-plus career working alongside an impressive (and often exclusive) clientele.

In fact, Sally's Co-creative Leadership education is a global first leadership curriculum that specifically focuses on the sustainability element of personal and professional transformation for high-level leaders who are fed up with wasting millions of dollars and countless man-hours on training and development that doesn't last.

Therefore, if you are a CEO, C-Suite executive, an executive overseeing a team, an entrepreneur, a politician, a millionaire, or a billionaire looking for sustainable personal and/or professional transformation, look no further than Sally Anderson.

When you do, be prepared to achieve unprecedented 'sustainable' RESULTS!

Annemarie Cross - CEO and Founder of Ambitious Entrepreneur Podcast Network and Industry Thought Leader Academy, and author of Industry Thought Leader: From Invisible to Influential (and Profitable) with a Podcast. – Melbourne, Australia

Sally Anderson creates personal and group transformations, with results that last and have impact, making Sally the absolute real deal. As a CEO and entrepreneur pushing a tough game, Sally transitioned us from default-based behaviours, barriers, disempowered thinking, and dysfunctional relationships to give way to focus, power-to-power conversations, and results. Sally works with CEOs and high-profile leaders to lead their organisation and elevate teams, bring them on the same page, and achieve results, including with some tough personalities, doubters, and blockers. The bigger the blocker, the bigger the transformation. She is superb one-on-one with individuals seeking personal and professional breakthroughs; she had a big impact on my life on key decisions, and I've witnessed her to do the same for others, in a sustainable way. She is powerful and empathic, impossible to deny. Sally is the top of her game, undisputed, and I will continue to benefit and enjoy working with her.

Helen Jarman – CEO of Activ Group, Founder of Ecoactiv Digital Platform to activate the Circular Economy Platform, Supply Chain, Reverse Logistics & Product Stewardship – Melbourne, Australia

Notes

equan